FOLLOWING JESUS IN AFRICA

by

Vivian Hutchison

Chandler Books

To my husband, Dave,
who constantly encouraged me
to write this book.

Special Edition
presented by the
Laymen's Evangelical Mission
P.O. Box 2001
Akron, Ohio 44309-2001

Published by Chandler Books in Mogadore, Ohio
Printed in the United States of America
Type set in 11 point ITC New Baskerville,
printed on acid-free paper with more than
50% recycled fibers, meeting the guidelines
for permanence and durability of the Committee
on Production Guidelines for Book Longevity
of the Council on Library Resources.

Library of Congress Card Catalogue No. 93-73981

ISBN 1-878893-44-0

PREFACE

Serving the Lord in Africa was almost like a dream happening to someone else and, yes, we literally DID pinch one another at times to see if we would wake up!

It opened our eyes in so many ways to the wonder and awesomeness of God and yet also to His practical side of faithfulness and sometimes miraculous guidance and supply!

We felt as if we'd been cut off from the world that we knew and set 'back in time' in another world with another people whom God loved very much and wanted to reach IF we would only allow HIM to guide us.

Writing about it has also warmed my heart and been a double blessing as it brings out the details again and God has revealed a small facet of HIS side of these stories. That's been a wonderful surprise!

Our thanks to our home church, The Chapel, in Akron, Ohio, for their support and prayers. Without their prayers, as well as the prayers of our family and friends, these events would never have happened!

My thanks also to my husband, Dave, with whom I've shared not only Africa, but 47 great years of life together. Our thanks also to our children: Kaye and her husband, Ernie; Dave and his wife, Vicki. They never tried to say or do anything to discourage us, even at our age, from following the Lord to the 'ends of the earth' as He led us.

Most of all we thank the Lord for allowing two nobodies, a welder and a homemaker, to experience the joy of serving Him in a fascinating place like Africa!

CONTENTS

1
FOLLOWING JESUS

Have not I commanded thee? Be strong and of a good courage; be not afraid, neither be thou dismayed: for the Lord thy God is with thee withersoever thou goest. Joshua 1:9

God used this command to strengthen my husband, Dave, and me as we prepared to follow His 'call' on our lives to serve Him in Swaziland, South Africa. We felt so cowardly and inadequate to face such scary things as jungle, wild animals (in my case, especially spiders and snakes) and savage, Zulu-speaking people. How could we, a welder and a homemaker, serve the Lord in such a place as that?

Many questions and fears pounded at us as we made all the preparations to obey His leading.

The words, "have not I commanded you," jolted into our minds over and over until they came alive. God was speaking to us *specifically*, NOT just to faintly encourage us, but COMMANDING us to be strong and unafraid because He, Almighty God, would be *with us* wherever we would go!

The emphasis of His spirit, through this verse and others that will be shared, brought stronger faith to trust God as He led us into a whole new era of 'following Him', which for us, has turned out to be a most delightful and rewarding ongoing daily walk.

PRAYER: Dear Lord, dispel our daily fears and doubts. Replace them with great expectation and trust in YOU, our Almighty God, Who promises to be *with us wherever we go!*

2

WILL GOD SUPPLY OUR NEEDS?

But my God shall supply all your need according to His riches in glory by Christ Jesus. Phil. 4:19

It was about to be our first time out on the mission field and the needs seemed insurmountable. Faith, strength, courage, health, financial support, food, housing, transportation, language barrier, ministry needs, these were just a beginning list of essential requirements flooding our minds! Was God in this? Would He supply these needs—

All financial requirements were met *overnight* as our home church's mission committee voted to supply our *full* support and transportation costs!

We had assumed that a grass-roofed mud hut would be our home but instead, found a very nice, large stucco house filled with the furniture of a furloughing missionary family.

Another departing missionary sold us her used but efficient VW bug for a price we could manage.

To our great surprise many people in Swaziland spoke English as a second language. We were thankful and amazed. What more could we ask?

As this story unfolds, you will see that faith, strength, courage, health, and ministry needs were a matter of God's *daily* miraculous provision in fulfillment of His promises and in answer to the faithful prayers of the many brothers and sisters in Christ and family members back home who had such a tremendous part in all that happened!

PRAYER: Dear Father, thank You for the creative and miraculous ways that You provide for our many needs, stretching our faith and trust as we follow You!

3
YES, AFRICA IS GOOD!

. . . and God saw that it was good. Gen. 1:25

The impression that all of Africa was totally jungle, wild animals and savages was quickly dispelled as we reached South Africa and our destination: the small, independently ruled country of Swaziland.

God had spread rugged mountains everywhere and lavished them with beautiful flowering trees and plants in a semi-tropical climate. It was so lovely yet primitive that we were constantly aware of God's creative beauty.

Although trees were plentiful, there were no jungles in Swaziland. Wild animals, for the most part, had to be seen on Game Reserves and the Swazi people were NOT savage. In fact, to our great relief, delight, and in answer to prayer, we found them, generally, to be gentle, friendly, and receptive—a handsome, mellow brown, pleasant people who quickly found a *special* place in our hearts!

How needlessly we had worried and feared the unknown future and circumstances that God was bringing into our lives!

Words are useless to explain the joy and love for God that filled our hearts as the *blessings* He had in store for us unfolded!

PRAYER: Thank You, Lord, for Your unspeakable goodness! Help us to put our hand in Yours that we may follow You into *blessings unknown!*

4
EVEN WE CAN BE FISHERS OF MEN?

Follow Me, and I will make you fishers of men. Matt. 4:19

Hardly had we unpacked (after just a week in Swaziland) when I was asked to share a Bible lesson in a nearby primary school. Although thrilled for this opportunity, I was more than apprehensive about speaking here for the first time and through an interpreter. There was only a short time for preparation and God kept me on my knees desperately seeking His guidance as to *what* lesson to present and *how* as I would face these Swazi children.

As I prayed, the verse, "Follow Me and I will make you fishers of men," filled my mind until I wondered if *this* was the lesson I was to give. I searched and found that very lesson on flannelgraph (left in the house by the former missionary).

The little school was within 5 kilometers but situated on a steep mountain without a road. Selinah (an African lady who was to be my interpreter) and I wobbily wound our way up the side of the mountain in the little VW, greeted by the unfamiliar sound of young Africans singing.

One-hundred-twenty (beaming but ragged) children packed the one-room school house, standing with bare feet on a cold cement floor. Their two young teachers stood alongside. Rickety benches were the *only* furnishings. There were NO desks, not even for the teachers. Education is not free in Swaziland so the students who are able to pay are usually enthusiastic learners no matter how difficult the conditions!

My heart swelled with God's love for them as I excitedly shared (with the help of Selinah and the flannel graph) the passage in Math. 4:17-20.

Midway through, I became frightened by a Swazi man on horseback who rode up to the door and shouted in

Siswati. I could hardly speak, expecting to be stopped by force. But as I prayed silently, the man rode off and we continued.

As the lesson closed, God's word again flooded my thoughts—"Follow Me, and I will make you fishers of men." I also had the unmistakable impression that I was to give an invitation *right then* for them to receive Jesus into their hearts. This seemed impossible on my very first visit!

Scared but obedient, I followed the Lord's leading and carefully explained the gospel—simply telling them that *all* people are sinners, even *children*, and that God sent Jesus, His Son, to die on the cross to pay the penalty for our sins and that Jesus is the ONLY way to heaven. God guided the words as I invited them to believe and receive Him as their Savior and Lord. In response, every child and both teachers stood and prayed to receive Christ into their lives!

I felt weak with thankfulness and joy at God's unspeakable goodness in drawing these precious souls to Himself on the very first opportunity that was given.

To our relief, the teachers informed us that the horseback rider was shouting a message about an important meeting for the people in that community. They invited Selinah and I back to share every week from then on and we had the delight of discipling the children and teachers to the point of a Christmas program in which *they* 'shared' so their *parents* could hear about Jesus.

The 'results' that day confirmed God's specific leading in every way and literally opened the way for me to trust His guidance and to follow Him so that He could make even *me* a fisher of men.

PRAYER: Oh Lord, thank You for the joy of your promise that even *we* can become fishers of men. No matter how scared or how weak or how unable we feel, YOU can DO it if we will follow YOU!

5
THE GARDEN OF EDEN

... and God shall give ... Read Deut. 6:10

As the days unfolded in this beautiful place, we began to realize that this mission station must resemble the Garden of Eden in all of its splendor.

Our back yard was filled with delicious oranges, grapes, and strawberries as well as lovely flowering trees and plants. Our eyes beheld beauty in every direction. A garden of vegetables was planted throughout the middle of the compound with banana and guava trees also plentiful.

The fruit flavors tasted so different when picked from a tree rather than being purchased in a market back home in the States. It was such a treat!

Although Swaziland has mild three-month long winters (June, July, and August) the rest of the year is semi-tropical, making the growing season lengthy.

One of our concerns before arrival was food. How would we ever find food that would be palatable to meet our needs?

PRAYER: Thank You, Lord, that *today* You *still* supply the physical needs of Your children even as You supplied 'manna' to the Israelites.

6
ABIDING IN HIM

If ye abide in Me, and My words abide in you, ye shall ask what ye will, and it shall be done unto you. John 15:7

The thrill of following Jesus to become a "fisher of men" soon had the added realization that "following" was to mean *more* than just *going* where He led. It also meant following His example of life. Abiding in Him and letting Him abide in me was to lead me into a deep desire to live a more holy life. The prayer to hate sin and become more Christlike became a constant request. The Africans had a chorus that said it all, "I want to be more and more like Jesus."

A strange language and different culture made it apparent that following Jesus would also mean a great need to be sensitive to His leading as to *what to say and when and how.* There was so much that He wanted to teach me about following Him.

Many nights of prayer on the hardwood floor are still precious times to remember. John 3:30, "He must increase, but I must decrease," filled my heart and mind often. I felt like a grain of sand, tiny, so inconsequential, yet that did my heart *good* because it put God in His true *gigantic* perspective. He answered my feelings and thoughts with a verse, "For He knoweth our frame; He remembereth that we are dust." (Ps. 103:14) I was thrilled that He would communicate! Yes, dust is much smaller than sand! My thoughts were still too high of myself. It was a great blessing and privilege to pray prostrate before Almighty God in close communion, love, tears and even laughter. Whatever might happen in this new and exciting adventure would not compare with the fellowship part of following Him!

PRAYER: Lord, thank You for the precious relationship with Yourself that You promise and give to ALL who truly seek to follow You.

7
GOD'S LOVE

For God so loved the world, that He gave His only begotten Son, that whosoever believeth in Him should not perish, but have everlasting life. John 3:16

All of these lessons from the Lord were bringing

the added wonderful blessing of drawing me nearer to Him. The word of God became more precious and alive every day, and along with that came a great hunger and unquenchable thirst for Him!

It seemed that time was suspended during many nights of prayer. As He drew me closer, I began to experience the agony God bears for those without Christ. I would find myself agonizing in prayer for them—great numbers of people—some that I knew, but mostly they were multitudes of strangers. Even as I suffered in prayer, deep within was the awareness that *this* was HIS *burden.* THIS was how God ached for people who have not yet believed and received Jesus Christ as their Savior and Lord! A weakness would come over me from the agony of His grief.

Up until that time, I thought I understood God's love. But never could I have really known the depth of His *love* without having experienced the depth of His agonizing *grief* for the lost.

Then I understood why God could actually send His only Son to *die* so that we might be saved and be able to be with Him forever throughout eternity. God's love is boundless and *unfathomable!*

PRAYER: Dear Father, we can't thank You enough for the love you have toward us that brings You such grief and that caused You to send Your precious Son as the *free* and *only* way to Heaven.

NOTE: Dear friend—God loves each us beyond all description! He loves YOU! Receive the endless love He offers you by repenting of sin and by believing and receiving His Son, Jesus, into *your* heart and life now. By that simple act of faith and trust, YOU can begin walking daily in the depth of God's perfect love!

8
KIDS EVERYWHERE

Read Mark 10:28-30: . . . he shall receive an hundredfold now in this time, houses, and brethren, and sisters, and mothers, and children. (verse 30)

Leaving our family behind had been the difficult part of following Jesus to Africa! I had to come to grips with that finally, late one night—praying and crying but placing each special family member into God's loving care. The peace of mind that we could trust Him to watch over them and that everything would be OK finally came.

The actual ministry of this mission station was a Christian high school and elementary school so there were children everywhere! It wasn't long before groups of these students were meeting for Bible Studies in our home. Five groups in all met weekly, each at a different level of spiritual growth. The challenges and blessings were many as we discovered that children are the same the world over. God's love and His Word, along with attention from a 'grandpa' and 'grandma', helped bring a close relationship with them.

God truly kept us busy with our new African family. The first time I was asked to speak to the elementary students on the station, I found 400 little kids jammed into the chapel. The aisles, all benches, and even the *platform* were covered completely with kids all loudly singing Christian songs in Siswati! There was hardly room for my feet and *no place* to put the flannelgraph. How exciting it was to minister to such eager listeners!

Again, by God's grace and by His Spirit, many of these 'little ones' received Jesus into their lives that day. It was a foretaste of countless opportunities and joys to come as we served the Lord in that place.

PRAYER: Oh Lord, how glad we are that we can still trust You TODAY to be faithful to Your promises whatever the circumstances as we follow You!

9

YESTERDAY, TODAY, AND FOREVER

Jesus Christ the same yesterday, and today, and forever. Heb. 13:8

The beauty of Swaziland was breathtaking. It was primitive and rugged but so lovely.

Gorgeous Birds of Paradise grew beside our doorstep. Jack-O-Randa lined the dirt roads of our compound. (These were huge, lilac colored *trees* instead of bushes like back home.) Flaming red Poinsettia *trees* grew all over and bloomed for several months!

Flowering bushes were everywhere, each in a different eye-catching color. Words can hardly describe the beautiful scene in every direction. We often literally thought this *had* to be a dream. It just didn't seem possible that a country this primitive and beautiful could be real in the urban, mechanized, modern world of today! It seemed as though following Jesus to this place had led us *back in time*.

One especially attractive bush grew next to our dining room window. Its delicate purple, blue, and white petals were exquisite! It was called Yesterday, Today, and Forever. We never tired of gazing at its unusual beauty and freshness! It reminded us of the beauty and wonder and exquisiteness of the Lord Jesus Christ, the ONLY one Who *is or ever will be* the SAME yesterday, today, and FOREVER!

PRAYER: Thank You, Lord, for the comfort of knowing that You never change. You are ALWAYS the *same* compassionate, understanding, forgiving, all-knowing, and loving Person. We APPRECIATE and LOVE You!

10
THE SPIDER

Be careful for nothing; but in every thing by prayer and supplication with thanksgiving let your requests be made known unto God. And the peace of God, which passeth all understanding, shall keep your hearts and minds through Christ Jesus. Phil. 4:6,7

Spiders, as I mentioned before, were near the top of my list of things to fear and even to run from. And, of all things, *that* was the very thing we encountered the *first night* right beside our bedroom door! It was the largest, ugliest, furriest monster spider we had ever laid eyes on! Even worse, it *disappeared* before we could do away with it and right in the hall by our bedroom. I was aghast to say the least!

After all the excitement of arrival, meeting the other missionaries (twenty one) and a preliminary survey all around, it was finally time to turn in.

As tired as I was, the *last* thing I wanted to do was sleep in this room where that monstrous spider might be! But it was the *only* room with a *bed* and all the floors were uncovered hardwood so we were forced into it.

After praying together, Dave THOROUGHLY inspected every inch of the room and bed and we settled down.

However, I quickly pulled the sheets *tight* over and around my head and body and PRAYED about everything I could think of concerning spiders, snakes, animals, bugs, heat, sickness and all other *fearful* things that came to mind. Truthfully, behind it all, was the looming question, "Lord, what have You gotten us into?"

God must've heard my desperate cry, for His peace began to settle over me. The jet lag and travel weariness caught me up into a sound sleep.

We woke to the bird sounds and beauty of an African morning without having been bitten, eaten, or carried off by that spider or anything *else* after all!

The peace God gave me that night certainly passed all understanding because from that time on I was really *not* fearful. It was as if my hand was in the Lord's as I followed Him. His closeness dispelled my fears.

Altogether, we saw *three* of those spiders over a two year period in that house. Dave was able to get two. Whether one was still *loose* or if we had seen one of them twice was always an interesting question?????

God ably *replaced* that GIANT fear which could've ruined every day in Africa, with an unbelievable peace!

PRAYER: Dear Father, what would we ever do if You did not hear our prayers and take away our fears? Please help some fearful person TODAY. Thank You for caring so much!

11
THE LADIES' RETREAT

I beseech you therefore, brethren, by the mercies of God, that ye present your bodies a living sacrifice, holy, acceptable unto God, which is your reasonable service. Romans 12:1

Dave came bounding breathlessly into the house eager to tell me that Reverend Gamedze, pastor of the Mission Church, had invited us to speak for six hours at an African ladies' retreat.

It was exciting because Dave had never even *attended* a *ladies'* retreat before and, although each of us had spoken individually, this would be the first time to speak TOGETHER with interpreters.

The retreat would be at Bethel where Malla Moe, the colorful, fruitful, first missionary to Swaziland, had lived and ministered until her death. Malla and Bethel were already special to us because of all we'd heard.

In the week we had to prepare, hours of prayer for direction led us to choose to share The Navigator Wheel,

a discipling concept that has also help
find Christ as their Savior. If only th
would make it plain to *Swazi* ladies!

That early morning of the retreat
African time is very *different* than real ti
many ladies who'd spent the night tog
but, although it was time to begin
program, we were told the ladies had just   ... eating
breakfast. We were led to a mud-walled building where
inside we saw, for the first time really, the poor, humble
conditions of the people. Our hearts melted at the sight
of the ladies *lying* in straw on a dirt floor eating a kind
of 'cream of wheat' mixture out of basins with their
hands. We felt God's love reaching out to them as we
moved among them shaking hands. It didn't matter that
their hands were covered with breakfast—nothing could
stop the need to touch and to love them!

Later, as we shared The Wheel, they seemed so attentive and hungry for the Word. Not understanding, but
determined to follow Jesus and OBEY whatever He led
us to do or to say, we felt specifically guided to give an
invitation *halfway* through the message instead of at the
finish. God's love poured through to them and many
ladies came forward crying. Some crawled on their
hands and knees to give their lives to Jesus while others
came for rededication.

That day was such a tremendous blessing and Jesus
stamped in our minds *again*, so clearly, that if we would
follow HIM, He would make *even us* "fishers of men" for
His honor and glory!

PRAYER: Dear Lord, thank You, thank You, for letting
us have a part in Your plan to reach a lost world.

The key to living a victorious, Spirit-filled Christian life is Jesus Christ as the Center and Lord of all we do. With Christ in control, life is balanced and effective. The Wheel illustrates this Christ-centered life.

CHRIST THE CENTER – Gal. 2:20; John 15:5; Col. 1:27

OBEDIENCE TO CHRIST – John 14:21; Rom. 12:1,2; Lu. 6:46

THE WORD – I Pet. 2:2; II Tim. 3:16,17; Josh. 1:8

PRAYER – Matt. 7:7; Phil. 4:6,7; John 15:7

FELLOWSHIP – Matt. 18:20; Heb. 10:24,25; I John 1:3

WITNESSING – Matt. 4:19; Rom. 1:16; I Pet. 3:15

12
THE TRUMPET

For My thoughts are not your thoughts, neither are your ways my ways, saith the Lord. For as the heavens are higher than the earth, so are My ways higher than your ways, and my thoughts than your thoughts. Iaiah 55:8,9

Dave was so busy serving the Lord as the Maintenance Superintendent of Franson Christian High School, organizing the work and the workers, to accomplish all the tasks involved on a one-thousand acre mission station. All of the high school and elementary school buildings as well as the houses for the missionary teachers needed care. He would designate, sometimes *illustrate,* and often 'pitched in' himself to help his crew of twenty to forty Africans.

Every morning the English-speaking cook would interpret for Dave to be able to share a Bible devotional with the workers. A close bond and mutual respect began to develop between them all. It was an answer to prayer!

My husband is a certified welder by trade, having welded steam pipes in schools, hospitals, factories, power houses, and several nuclear plants, along with many other welding opportunities back home. So he was more than happy to find a welding machine as part of the equipment in the Mission's shop building!

One day an excited African man, in full Swazi national dress, including hair feathers, shield and spear, strode into the workshop with an *ancient,* well-used trumpet. With the help of body language, it became understood that it was in desperate need of repair. The Swazi gentleman, who turned out to be a community official, was trying Dave as a *last resort* to bring new life to his beloved instrument.

In a way, it was like the old-time mission stories of a doctor having to prove himself by healing a sick child or person. Dave was on the 'spot'. Everyone watched as he tried, for the first time in his life, to *heal* a sick, delicate *trumpet*. Fortunately, there was an acetylene torch and some silver solder for him to begin what turned out to be a successful operation! When finished and after a few trial blasts, the trumpet sounded with a medley of beautiful songs echoing off the mountains as the Swazi official marched off happy and triumphant.

God, Who knows all, used this unusual experience as a stamp of approval for Dave and for his acceptance among the Swazi men, thereby opening doors and opportunities for relationships and ministry among them.

PRAYER: Thank You, heavenly Father, that in Your unusual way, and in answer to the prayers of many, You find ways to open doors so that your servants can accomplish Your plans as they follow You.

13

MALLA MOE

Read Romans 10:13-15,17: How beautiful upon the mountains are the feet of him that bringeth good tidings, that publisheth peace; that bringeth good tidings of good, that publisheth salvation. Isaiah 52:7

It was some time after the ladies' retreat when, unexpectedly, we discovered a book about the life of Malla Moe. Excitedly we borrowed it and could hardly wait to read it every evening.

Malla Moe was a thirty-year-old, single, Norwegian woman when she arrived to serve the Lord as the *first* missionary to Swaziland. Her life and love for the Lord and the Swazi people soon brought her a ministry among them unequaled by anyone since. It was a rewarding, but difficult life which eventually led her to travel over the mountains in a specially made covered wagon pulled by sixteen donkeys. This enabled her to live with, and evangelize, and teach these people she loved so dearly. God blessed with 'fruit' and groups of Christians grew out of her ministry across the country until there were even several mission stations established including Franson Christian High School as well as Bethel, her home and headquarters.

Malla Moe ministered throughout Swaziland until her death at 90, which was 13 years *before* our arrival. It was heartwarming as we met many Africans who had become Christians as a result of her ministry. Hundreds were now even in full-time service for the Lord!

As the ministry expanded, Malla would sort of 'orient' each new missionary or missionary couple upon their arrival getting to know them and helping them adjust.

We were fascinated to learn that one of the first things she felt led to do was to thoroughly pray into their lives Mathew 4:19, "Follow Me, and I will make you fishers of men," claiming this promise from God for their lives and ministry in Swaziland!

Knowing how the Lord had used that same verse in *my* life the very first week with the children at Galiel and soon after at the Ladies' Retreat at Bethel, we couldn't help but realize that the Lord *had* specifically led Malla Moe in her 'orientation' and prayers for the new missionaries. And now, without Malla Moe's presence, He was *still* using that verse to powerfully guide new missionaries to follow Him and become "fishers of men!"

PRAYER: Dear Lord, may we each continue to trust Your guidance TODAY as Malla did in those days, and follow YOU as she did in a simple way, but with extraordinary results. "For *with God* NOTHING shall be impossible!" Luke 1:37

14
THE CLINIC – I

Read Mathew 9:1-7: It is of the Lord's mercies that we are not consumed, because His compassions fail not. They are new every morning: great is Thy faithfulness. Lamentations 3:22,23

After we had 'settled in' at Mhlosheni and began to 'see' with open eyes and to 'hear' with open ears, I began to notice large groups of patients waiting for treatment at a Government Clinic next door to the Mission. They looked so hopeless.

Realizing they were evidently *physically* ill and wondering how many were *spiritually* ill, I started praying fervently for them wishing that we could speak Siswati to tell them that Jesus cared and of His saving power!

Soon thereafter, the Deputy Headmaster (assistant principal) of the high school, Mr. George Villakati, and his wife, Bongi, rode into the nearest town with us. As we passed the clinic, I confided my desire to share the Gospel with these waiting people. To our amazement, Bongi, who was a *nurse*, explained that she was to become the *person in charge* of that clinic starting the following Monday. She invited me to come every weekday, with an interpreter, to minister to them! George suggested that some willing students could interpret during the school library period. We were overwhelmed by the sense of God's goodness in answering this prayer!

It wasn't difficult to find 'willing' interpreters in this Christian school and that Monday morning, during library period, we began what was to become a *daily* blessing of ministering to these waiting crowds.

Usually three students helped. They would all sing in their beautiful harmonious way and invite the people to join in a chorus. We'd pray, then one of the students would give a testimony of how he or she had come to know Christ. Another would interpret the Gospel message for me. We realized constantly the Lord's Power and Presence as He drew many of these dear sick people to Himself!

We would move among them after the message and invitation, praying personally for their requests, answering questions, encouraging them however possible until the library period ended and my interpreters had to return to class.

God's blessings at the clinic made each day a rewarding challenge and brought close relationships with many students as they took turns serving the Lord in this way.

PRAYER: Heavenly Father, THANK YOU for caring so much for each of us. Wrap Your love and compassion around someone in need TODAY. Help someone to seek You and FIND You and FOLLOW you!

Vivian shares with patients at the clinic,
Franson Christian High School students interpreting.

15
THE CLINIC – II

Read John 4:1-29: The woman then left her waterpot, and went her way into the city. John 4:28

Every day was a different challenge at the clinic with new people waiting for treatment. Some would stand, others sat on the ground, and often the most seriously ill would *lay on the grass.*

Our hearts would soften as we approached them. It was such a privilege to 'share' among the ill of all ages. Unknown to them, the love of God surrounded that place. The students and I sensed His Presence and concern!

A Swazi kraal (home) made up of several mud and thatched buildings—one for cooking and a separate building for each wife and her children.

As we shared the Gospel one day and then spread out to talk to people, one young woman drew my attention. She was resting on the grass nursing her *twins*. She had questions. With the interpreter's help we could converse and soon she disclosed that, although she'd heard our gospel message and knew she needed Christ in her life, she had NOT received Him during our invitational prayer. But now, she wanted to commit her life to Him and she DID as we prayed together with her.

Immediately, after receiving Christ as her Savior, she began to cry out for her family, sobbing that she had five brothers who were lost and begging me to share the Gospel with *them* at her home RIGHT NOW!

How could I possibly refuse? Of course we would do it. I ran back to our house and in the *front* door just as Dave was coming in the back door asking, "What's for lunch?"

"There's no time for lunch today," I answered and then shared quickly the woman's burden to reach her family for Christ.

Without delay we all gathered into the VW and drove to her home on a nearby mountainside. One of her brothers was standing by their house gazing hopelessly. Three more of the brothers were also home.

While explaining, she gathered them together and placed mats on the ground. Although we had not *seen* any houses or families close by, suddenly people were drifting toward us until there was a congregation seated on the mats!

Following Jesus that day gave Dave and I the blessing of seeing four of the brothers, as well as others, commit their lives to the Lord as His Spirit moved in that place!

PRAYER: Lord, have we often failed to recognize the different kinds of 'women at the well' who've crossed our paths? Forgive us and help us to be sensitive as You want to reach out to them and their loved ones! Amen.

16
THE CLINIC – III

Train up a child in the way he should go: and when he is old, he will not depart from it. Proverbs 22:6. Come unto me, all ye who labour and are heavy laden and I will give you rest. Matt. 11:28

On a coolish rainy day while speaking again with people at the clinic, a very sad-eyed elderly lady with a huge bundle tied to her back wanted to speak through the interpreter to me. Tears rolled over wrinkles as she heartbrokenly told us of her only son's mistreatment of her. His unkindness had ended that day by beating her and throwing her and all of her belongings out of his home. A Christian and widow, without any other family, she was terrified with no place to go.

My five feet height seemed tall as I stood beside this broken woman with a burden on her back and on her heart. She was soaked with rain as I laid a hand on her shoulder to pray for God's intervention in this desperate situation.

Nomsa, my translator, and I felt the heartache ourselves as we invited her to come to the mission station, at least temporarily. But, maybe because of pride, she refused and walked off sadly.

We continued praying for her until weeks later she appeared in the crowd at the clinic again. She seemed transformed and was eager to tell us how God had answered prayer as she found a friend that day who gave her shelter. Then, her son, who had been a Christian since childhood, had wrestled with his conscience and ill treatment of his mother and finally, asked for God's forgiveness. He had rededicated his life and searched for and found his mother asking for forgiveness and had returned her to his home!

She told how her family's lives were changed and how peace and love had entered in. They were now following the Lord.

PRAYER: Oh God, together we seek Your Divine Hand upon families and even marriages TODAY asking You to mend broken relationships, restoring unselfish love and kindness that will bind families and homes together around the world! Amen.

17
THE CLINIC – IV

Beware of false prophets which come to you in sheep's clothing, but inwardly they are ravening wolves. Matt. 7:15

Rudely interrupting our message at the clinic one morning was a very young girl about twelve years old. Stepping right up beside us she loudly began preaching false doctrine in Siswati! The students with me questioned her but she kept on *shouting* her cultic message to the crowd.

Even though she was a child, it was very difficult to get her quieted down so that we could finish our gospel message. But finally, she retreated and God worked in the hearts of our listeners in spite of this interruption!

It was overwhelming to think of this *child* being so *bold* to speak out her *false* doctrines and to try to 'wrestle' the gospel away from that group! Especially since we *Christian adults* are often too weak and shy to share our truths of *God's Word* even just person to person!

PRAYER: God, help us to be STRONG in *our* faith and BOLD in *our* witness and to be *fruitful, effective witnesses* for You and for Your glory! Amen.

18
THE CLINIC – V

Read II Cor. 4:1-7: For we preach not ourselves, but Christ Jesus the Lord; and ourselves your servants for Jesus' sake.

Every day at the clinic was a SPECIAL blessing from the Lord. It became more and more evident how *much* God cared for these dear people as He continued to open their hearts to respond to His word!

A very exceptional brown face with intense bright *blue* eyes stood out as I shared the Word one morning, along with my students. She appeared several times watching and listening intently, then finally spoke, through my helpers, to ask me to come and preach at her church on a nearby mountain. It seemed that the preacher in her church was her *own son*. But she sadly disclosed that he was NOT preaching the gospel to them. She begged *me* to come and speak to the congregation! It was a surprising request but she insisted that she'd already asked her son and he also was inviting me to share in their church.

She gave directions to my interpreters, but in a *Swazi* way, which turned out to be too vague for me to follow. Several times I tried to find her church but failed. Every few months she would return and ask me to PLEASE come. I'd get instructions again, would try again, but to no avail.

Finally, a bearded Swazi man knocked on our door one Monday along with a student interpreter. I discovered he was this lady's son and had come to take me to his church!

Leaving a note for my husband, I met this man at the clinic a few minutes later. He was to bring an interpreter. But as the two got into the VW I was startled to see that this girl was the very one I'd seen literally dragged into a car and taken home because of *demon possession* just a week before!

My heart flopped unsteadily as I realized that I (*alone*) was about to drive to a remote place with a strange man who couldn't speak English and a demon possessed girl! GOD FORBID! But they were already in and the girl was giving directions. I swallowed my heart, prayed silently, *desperately,* and drove—discovering as the poor little VW ploughed along, *why* I had never been able to find this church. We climbed a nearby mountain sideways without a road, going through a stream and then a river and over rocks, through high weeds and steep cow pastures until we reached the top and came to a clearing. There we found a primitive little church and a fairly large square building used as a school.

In the Lord's wonderful timing, the doors of the school opened. I reached quickly into the glove compartment for 200 Siswati gospel tracts I had just purchased. I delightedly shook hands hurriedly with and gave a tract to *each* excited student as they came flying out the door.

The *last* child received the *last* tract! It was amazing that the Lord's leading brought our *arrival* instantaneous with the school's *dismissal* and 200 tracts would now be shared with families spread out over that mountainside! And I was STILL whole. The man WAS the preacher son and the girl was evidently *healed* of demon possession.

PRAYER: THANK YOU, Lord Jesus, for the wonders that come while following You! How very, very GREAT THOU ART!

(continued)

19

THE CLINIC – VI

Trust in the Lord with all thine heart; and lean not unto thine own understanding. In all thy ways acknowledge Him, and He shall direct thy paths. Proverbs 3:5,6

The very next Sunday, I was to preach in that little church on the mountain top. Wondering why God would put a *woman* in this pulpit, I asked my husband to come also and prayerfully we looked to the Lord for guidance and *tried* not to lean on our own understanding. We trusted Him to show us which of us should *really* preach and which should give testimony asking His great blessing upon the congregation! By this time, Christmas was approaching and the Birth of Christ seemed to be the needed message as this could be the only opportunity to tell these people of Christ's coming and *why*.

This time Dave had the privilege of driving up that mountainside and as one of the large holes nearly gobbled up our VW, we saw a Swazi running toward us. Sudden fear subsided as he held out guava fruit, smiling and bowing as he came. Our hearts leaped with thanks and love for this unknown friend!

Such were the greetings and gifts waiting for us every so often as we wound our way up this rugged terrain. We felt so warmly welcome as we followed the Lord to this strange place and unusual opportunity.

The people were singing hymns joyfully as we reached the top of the mountain and entered the church with hearts pounding.

How *greatly* SURPRISED we were then to see that this congregation was *all* WOMEN and CHILDREN! The only man present was the preacher.

He and his mother had failed to tell me.

NOW WE UNDERSTOOD!

Thankful that God knows *everything*, we felt His presence in a wonderful way as I preached the blessed birth of Christ and what Christmas is all about to receptive women and children that morning with the help of a teacher translator! Dave shared his testimony and the response to the service was *rewarding*. The translator told us that all these people really have known about Christmas was to kill an animal, then have a celebration feast. It was, she said, their *first* time to ever hear the gospel.

We were touched when the ladies asked that we pray for their husbands to come to church and hear about Jesus. We knelt with all of the congregation immediately before the Lord and prayed together for

The primitive church on the mountaintop.

His Spirit to move in the men's hearts to bring them to church and to Himself. It was a precious time of prayer and fellowship bonding our lives with one another!

It was so *exhilarating!* However, the path back home seemed *more* treacherous than before. The VW tried its level best, but slid in the swollen river coming to rest on a huge, flat rock. We were just horrified as we waded around it in our 'Sunday clothes' to see what could be done. Just as desperation began, we heard the sound of people coming and there, as if from nowhere, were several Swazi men who, along with Dave, were able to slide the car off the rock and onto more solid ground in the river bed. The language barrier kept us from being

River crossed—we're on our way again.

able, verbally, to express our thanks. But the handclasps and smiles mutually filled that gap! GOD BLESS SUCH PEOPLE!

PRAYER: Lord Jesus, following You brings not only 'angels of mercy' such as the men who so willingly helped us but also brings people in NEED. Someone *right now* needs Your blessed Spirit to move in the heart of their husband or wife in a *mighty way* to bring them to Yourself! With all of our hearts we pray this for loved ones TODAY! Amen.

20
THE CLINIC – VII

Read Matt. 9:20-22: And behold, a woman, which was diseased with an issue of blood twelve years, came behind Him, and touched the hem of His garment. Matt. 9:20

One beautiful morning as a helper and I finished ministering at the clinic, a girl ran screaming up the road toward us! Then, pulling on our hands she wanted us to follow her.

Following Jesus that day took us running to a river bed about one-fourth mile behind the clinic. There in the middle of the shallow water was a young woman collapsed flat on her back sobbing in panic!

My translator ran back to the clinic to get assistance as I discovered this Swazi lady spoke English. She was hemorrhaging and very weak.

What a blessing it was to realize God's love and concern for her as I knelt beside her in the water, held her hand and PRAYED! God's peace quieted her and I began to tell her of His love for her and of His Son, the Lord Jesus Christ. She had heard of Him before but *now*, in her need, in the middle of a river, she prayed and asked Jesus into her heart!

As rescuers arrived to carry her to the clinic, I followed soaked but thrilled and thankful *again* that God cares so very much! He had met her need right where she was—just like the woman in Matthew 9.

PRAYER: Lord, someone today may be in physical need and panic, even though they may not be in a riverbed like the Swazi lady. Reach out and 'touch' them with Your helping and healing hand. May they experience Your loving care! Thank You, Lord. Amen

21
GOD PROVIDES 'FOLLOW UP'

Go ye therefore, and teach all nations, baptizing them in the name of the Father, and of the Son, and of the Holy Ghost: Teaching them all things whatsoever I have commanded you: and, lo, I am with you alway, even unto the end of the world. Matt. 28:19,20.

Shortly after arrival at Mhlosheni, it was evident that we needed 'follow up' materials in the Siswati language. In fact we had prayed about this even on the plane flying to Africa, asking God to supply that need. But questions and inquiring here and there had not brought results.

One quiet Sunday evening, a fellow missionary on the station, Bruce Britten, invited everyone to his house (down the street) for popcorn and to help him with a project. We all gathered to 'pitch in' discovering that his need was for helpers to collate the pages of a book he had just finished writing and mimeographing (with his wife, Carol's help).

It was exciting to find as the pages turned into books that what they had produced was "How To Become A Christian and How To Live The Christian Life." We could hardly wait to read it! Each page was written in *both* English and Siswati so that any Swazi could understand it, and was in excellent, sound doctrine. Their price was only 10c!

Once again God had answered prayer exceedingly and abundantly beyond what we could ask or think! (Eph. 3:20)

The Brittens were startled when Dave and I placed the first order that night requesting two hundred books! God, who had brought souls to Himself at Mhlosheni, had now also brought the perfect materials for 'follow up' written by His direction right there under our noses on the Mission Station.

It was a great delight from then on to be able to give out these books to everyone who received Christ and to anyone else who was genuinely interested and to have them widely distributed as God blessed our witnessing opportunities day by day at the clinic and in that community! There were always enough funds to buy the hundreds of books needed and Siswati New Testaments also.

"God is so Good" was the song and the statement in our hearts every day as He opened the way and we followed Him!

As of now, Bruce has written several books that are distributed in ten different languages and countries in Africa—soon also to be in India!

PRAYER: Lord, we thank You for Your miraculous supply at always the *perfect time*. May You provide exceedingly and abundantly for each one TODAY who is following You! Amen.

22
NOMSA & THABSILE

For God, who commanded the light to shine out of darkness, hath shined in our hearts, to give the light of the knowledge of the glory of God in the face of Jesus Christ. But we have this treasure in earthen vessels, that the excellency of the power may be of God, not of us. IICor. 4:6,7

Many of the students at Franson Christian High would do odd jobs for the school or for the missionaries in order to earn extra money. That's how we met Nomsa who came to help me wash walls. A delightful girl with stronger faith than any young Christian we had ever met anywhere!

As we grew better acquainted with Nomsa and her friend, Thabsile (also a very strong Christian), we learned of their deep desire to share Christ with others. But because of their youth (in Swazi culture it's a hindrance), they had few opportunities to share Christ's saving power.

Both girls spoke English well, and soon, as we began encouraging them, they launched out together visiting in kraals to proclaim the Gospel. People began to find Jesus Christ as their Savior and Lord! Nomsa and Thabsile had become 'home missionaries' overcoming the youth barrier and their own fears of inadequacy to reach out to people who needed to hear their message. God blessed their courage and obedience and used these young, 'earthen vessels' as "fishers of men."

These girls also worked in the mission school's garden. The time came when, instead of eating, they would even use their lunch periods to speak of Jesus to fellow workers.

In a short time God opened the way for Nomsa, Thabsile, and me to serve Him together in countless ways and circumstances!

PRAYER: Dear Lord, thank you for Nomsa and Thabsile and many others today who are like them, ready to serve You but feeling too young and inadequate. Bless and encourage and send them out with Your gospel and for Your honor and glory. Amen.

23
THE BURDEN GROWS GREATER

They that sow in tears shall reap in joy. He that goeth forth and weepeth, bearing precious seed, shall doubtless come again with rejoicing, bringing his sheaves with him. Psalm 126:5,6
The Lord is not willing that any should perish, but that all should come to repentance. II Peter 3:9

Although the days were getting fuller because ordinary daily tasks were harder in Africa, yet, in answer to the prayers of many folks back home, my strength seemed to abound!

No matter what the circumstances, it seemed that I needed less and less sleep but more and more time with God! Long, quiet hours in the night, flat on my face before the Lord in precious fellowship, brought strength to my soul and body and a love for Him that couldn't stop growing. The Bible became so alive that I began to read it on my knees out of deep respect.

God's promises stood out like neon signs and as days of *claiming* these promises went by, we experienced His fulfilling of them one by one, in extraordinary ways.

The realization came that God's word is actually THE UNDERSTATEMENT OF ALL TIME because He does so much *more* than He even promises, "abundantly above all that we ask or think, according to the power that worketh in us." (Eph. 3:20)

This part of "following Him," as we've tried to explain previously, brought a sense of seeing the world as He sees it and with that came a heavy, heavy burden for people without Christ! As this burden grew there were times of agonized sobbing until I could hardly bear it. Then, ever so gently, would come a reminder from the Lord that my agony was only a tiny part of the burden He carries.

One afternoon as this burden brought heavy tears, I ran out of our house to find Dave to pray for me but ran instead into another missionary who, when understanding the circumstances, prayed wisely for me. She asked that God would NOT take away this burden but that He would lead and direct me in such a way as to enable me to be a vessel for Him as HE reached out to the 'lost' with the saving power of His Son, Jesus Christ!

PRAYER: Dear Father, thank You for YOUR agonizing love and burden for the world. Reach out to someone today we pray! Amen.

24
WHAT ABOUT CHRISTMAS ?

. . . I am come that they might have life, and that they might have it more abundantly. John 10:10

The weather was getting warmer every day. New flowers were bursting out. The scenery was breathtaking and people began saying, "We can tell that Christmas is coming because it's getting so hot and all the flowers and bushes are blooming!"

To Dave and me (from Ohio), Christmas meant freezing cold, snow, and evergreens. This was a strange change!

But difference didn't matter. The excitement of Christmas began to set in! What would the celebration of Christ's birth be like in this culture?

Our missionary friends informed us that during this holiday the school was closed and the students and African teachers returned to their homes in other parts of Swaziland, causing the Mission Station to be deserted and lonely. Even the church was nearly empty without the two hundred boarding students in it.

We could not imagine a church that would not be full of worshipers at Christmas time, the perfect time for sharing the birth of Christ and no one to hear?

We began to pray that God would change that situation and bring a way to share the Gospel of Jesus Christ and FILL that church on Christmas Sunday.

There wasn't too much hope for such a thing until the idea burst through my mind that we should have a very SPECIAL Christmas program that would bring people from the surrounding area to hear abut Jesus!

Without the students it didn't seem possible, but Jerry Harpool, the headmaster of Franson Christian High School, thought he could get a film in Siswati about "The Lamb." The Swazi people who all had sheep, cows, and goats and were shepherds, would understand this portrayal of Christ. Jerry would also preach a message on the Love of Christ and George Vilikati (Jerry's African friend and the assistant principal) would translate.

The whole staff grew excited with the anticipation of Christmas at Mhlosheni!

PRAYER: Oh Lord, following You is the most exciting life! Please help someone to find Your abundant life for them TODAY!

(continued)

25
CHRISTMAS IS COMING – I

Call unto Me, and I will answer thee, and shew thee great and mighty things, which thou knowest not. Jeremiah 33:3

Now that the plan of what to do at Christmas was clear, our prayer was how to spread the news about the special program.

The idea that seemed most natural was for me to invite people every day at the clinic when I shared the Gospel. Also I needed to move around the area wherever groups of Swazis were gathered, informing them of the special Holiday program and asking them to PLEASE COME!

It was three weeks before Christmas—just enough time for everything to work out—HOPEFULLY!

Nomsa and Thabsile were thrilled to hear of our plans and eager to be my interpreters on this new venture.

With excitement, yet fear and trepidation, we started out the first day at the school chapel where we knelt together and prayed for God's divine guidance, protection, and blessing, asking to be filled with His love and compassion for these people.

Setting out in the little VW toward the clinic, we found the people very happy to hear of the special plans for Christmas (after we had first shared the Gospel and ministered to them). Their smiling faces and promises to come were a great encouragement to us as we drove on to find another group.

Across the road from Franson Christian High School was the post office and bus stop. In fact, those two places and the Mission really made up the whole town called Mhlosheni. But hundreds of people would gather there to get mail and wait for buses. Ladies were usually selling vegetables and fruit so that it was a very busy spot.

We pulled up there and with hearts in our throat we managed to get their attention, then launched out with our *special invitation*. We felt God's love flow through in telling them to please come and find out, on that day, what Christmas is all about. To our delight they were very interested and receptive promising to come. Surprisingly, they wanted to hear what Christmas was all about RIGHT NOW!

With great joy we told about the birth of Christ, His life, and the reason for His coming—the CROSS—and, as God led, we gave them the opportunity to believe and receive Jesus as their Savior and Lord! Many prayed and then talked to us personally.

Our hearts were full as we left that large crowd so THANKFUL for God's wonderful answer to prayer in opening this new opportunity to share His Son in this community.

We could never have imagined what lay ahead for us in the days to come as we followed our Lord in this new way!

PRAYER: Dear Father, give us Your ideas each day in Your creative, yet practical way, and fulfill your plans for each of us in Your Great Commission.

26
CHRISTMAS IS COMING! – II
THE STORE

For with God nothing shall be impossible. Luke 1:37

Around the corner from the clinic and back off the road was a primitive African store where the Swazi people could grind their mealies (corn) and buy bread as well as flour, sugar, and African-designed materials for clothing, etc.

It was raining but, amazingly, there was a crowd milling around this store. Again, as at the clinic, the hopelessness in their eyes and on their faces gripped our hearts! It compelled us to have courage again to get their attention and share about our special Christmas program. Faces lit up with interest and people promised to come.

But their need wouldn't let us go. They wanted to talk to us *personally*.

With thankful hearts for such a blessed opportunity, Nomsa and Thabsile took turns standing beside me holding an umbrella over our heads so I could read from my Bible while they translated every word.

The people lined up on both sides of us in the rain to personally hear the Gospel of Jesus Christ one by one under our umbrella. Their response was overwhelming!

So many prayed on the spot, others rededicated their lives to Christ! Some said they understood their need for Him but weren't ready for that commitment yet. Others needed time to think about it in order to understand more fully. ALL received Bruce Britten's book, "How to Become A Christian and How To Live The Christian Life." On the back of the books was my stamped address and each was given the invitation to my home to have questions answered or for prayer or whatever their ministry need. We loved them! They knew it! *God's love* flowed between us. It was gripping but wonderful to experience!

As Nomsa and Thabsila took turns interpreting for me, the other would move through the crowd answering questions, ministering, and also praying with more who received Christ.

God's saving Love reached down from Heaven that day as we followed Him to the little store!

But the episode was still not over . . . .

PRAYER: Oh, Lord, thank You that Your mercy and grace reach down to touch people's lives wherever they are—even in an African market place. Amen.

27
SYLVIA AT THE STORE – III

The Lord also will be a refuge for the oppressed, a refuge in times of trouble. And they that know thy name will put their trust in thee: for thou, Lord, hast not forsaken them that seek thee. Psalm 9:10

The rain kept pouring down on the waiting lines still standing on both sides of us at the store. More and more people were queing (lining up) to hear, personally, the Gospel of Jesus Christ! Hardly any of them carried umbrellas because they balanced large, heavy loads on top of their heads.

One pair of eyes were frightened as they'd meet mine and she nearly left the line several times. I was glad when her turn finally came to move under my umbrella to talk. She was wet, ragged, and obviously tormented, her eyes searching the crowd fearfully for someone that she was afraid of.

Her name was Sylvia. She listened longingly to the truths about Jesus—that He was God's very own Son sent to save the world—sent to save *Sylvia*. She wept as she heard. I reached out and hugged her wet shoulders.

She needed Jesus more than anything she said but could not pray to receive Him. As she spoke, two evil-looking men in a lorry (truck) were driving slowly through the crowd past us. Sylvia began to move now, frantically asking questions. Nomsa and I ran beside her answering, and suddenly she hopped into the back of the moving lorry telling us she wanted to pray. With muddy water slopping all over us from the puddles in the lane, we hurried along beside the lorry quickly helping Sylvia pray to receive Jesus into her heart and life, finishing just at the end of the lane. She waved with a joyful face as the lorry quickly pulled out on the mountain road.

Sylvia was gone but she *took Jesus with her!* He would never leave her nor forsake her! That comforting thought was with us as we trekked back through the rain and mud to the waiting lines of people.

My voice was growing weak but I was aware of God's strength and heart within to be able to continue sharing His love, personally, with such receptive and needy listeners.

It was thrilling as the Spirit of God moved in the hearts of people! In spite of the handicap of interpretation, the bond of His love and understanding drew us close. Following Jesus brings friends no matter what the language or racial barriers!

PRAYER: Dear God, we thank You that Your love reaches out to anyone in any circumstance at any time— because You can do ANYTHING! Even now strengthen Sylvia and ALL who came into Your family at the store, and touch the heart and life of some *reader* in need also.

(continued)

28

THE BUTCHERY
(AT THE STORE)

Therefore if any man be in Christ, he is a new creature: old things are passed away; behold, all things are become new. II Cor. 5:17

As the lines grew thinner, a man ran over several times to beg us to bring our message of Christ into the butchery building several yards away. We promised not to leave without sharing there.

The rain continued, but God's wonderful love was pouring down with the rain as we followed Him to the store that day!

By now we were wet and hoarse, but the waiting lines of people had been ministered to and we moved, under our umbrella, to the butchery. It was a small cement building without electricity and without a front door.

Stepping around toward the back door, Nomsa and I found the path blocked by many young Swazi men. They were in a circle, some on their knees, the rest standing, but all were excited and shouting! Our fear leaped instantly as we saw the center of attraction on the wet, sandy ground. A pair of dice! They were shooting crap! Now what? My heart sank but then Nomsa encouraged me to go ahead and announce the invitation to our special Christmas program. She called out for their attention in Siswati several times. Amazingly many of the young men, noticing the Bible in my hands, respectfully removed their hats and we stepped closer so they could hear in the rain.

With a smaller group now still on their knees shooting dice noisily at our feet, we invited those listening to come on Christmas to hear what Christmas is all about. Interest showed in their eyes. They said they wanted to come but could we PLEASE tell them NOW what Christmas is all about!

Our excitement was high as we shared the birth of Christ and even the events of the Cross while standing almost in the middle of that crap game. The several

A Swazi woman at the butchery with her baby *and* 10 gallons (80 pounds) of water on her head.

gamblers on their knees were oblivious to us but most of the crowd around them listened intently. Most bowed their heads and some of them *knelt in the mud* to pray and receive Christ as their Savior and Lord! Our hearts rejoiced as we talked, personally, to each new believer and gave them the book, "How To Become A Christian and How To Live The Christian Life." They left the crap game and we watched them move around in the crowd still at the store *sharing and reading* the books to others!

PRAYER: Thank You, Lord Jesus, that You still call rugged young men to yourself even in the middle of a crap game! Thank You for the courage You gave to these young Swazis to leave their old life and to follow You in a new life!

29
STILL AT THE BUTCHERY
(AT THE STORE)

For though I preach the gospel, I have nothing to glory of: for necessity is laid upon me; yea, woe is unto me, if I preach not the gospel! I Cor. 9:16 . . . warning every man, and teaching every man in all wisdom; that we may present every man perfect in Christ Jesus. Col. 1:28

There were a number of people in the butchery as we found our way inside. One of the butchers pointed to another and asked that we explain the gospel to him.

For the next ten minutes we answered his questions and then, thrillingly, he surrendered his life to Christ behind the meat counter with customers waiting! A smile lit up his face as his attention turned back to the waiting Swazis.

But then *they* also wanted to hear what this was all about. He encouraged them to gather together. Nomsa translated with all of her heart as we shared again God's plan of salvation with these eager listeners! Though we were wet, hoarse, and growing weary, the priceless message of Christ always brought renewed strength and enthusiasm to share it as long as God brought opportunities! Some of these customers became Christians also with a humbleness that showed their need and deep sincerity.

As we finished ministering, this time we drove back to the chapel, where we had begun the day in prayer together. This day could not end without thanking and praising God for all that He had done! Happiness and thankfulness far outweighed our weariness and we sang together, with vigor, "How Great Thou Art" and "To God Be the Glory."

PRAYER: Oh Lord, how truly GREAT You are! May all honor and glory be Yours forever!

30
CHRISTMAS IS GETTING CLOSER
(THE LITTLE VW)

Read II Timothy 4:1-5: Preach the word; be instant in season, out of season; reprove, rebuke, exhort with all longsuffering and doctrine. II Timothy 4:2

The little VW became a familiar sight in that community all up and down the surrounding mountains as we continued to extend our invitation to the special Christmas program. It was a delight that, nearly every time, we were also asked to explain, right on the spot, what Christmas is all about! The Spirit of God was working in the hearts and lives of the Swazi people and many were coming to Christ every day in answer to the prayers of all the folks back home and the prayers of the Swazi Christians in the church on the Mission Station. It was exciting!

It became a common happening to pull up at a busy spot and have people crowd the VW so that I couldn't even open my door to get out. Nomsa would lower her window and in Siswati would move them back from her side so that she could get out and come around the car to help me out to step into the crowd. Folks were so eager to hear our invitation and message. They wanted to come as close as possible seeking the warmth of God's love! He freely gave it and they felt it. So did Nomsa and I!

It was a joy to speak with the people also one on one whenever possible—praying for their needs and watching God bring joy and peace to their hearts and faces. Sadness and hopelessness were replaced with the love and hope of God. Nomsa and I often hated to leave them—the bonds would bind so quickly.

But the little VW had to move on to help us find someone else in need along the road or at a bus stop or in a field close to the road. Wherever there was a person to share with, it stopped. Malla Moe's wagon pulled by sixteen donkeys was named "The Gospel Wagon" (enquola evangeli). We began calling the VW "The *Little* Gospel Wagon."

It went up the mountains, over the rocks, through rivers, and bounced off many ruts. Cow pastures didn't stop it or cows on the road (called 'heavy traffic' in Swaziland). It was usually filled with music as Nomsa, Thabsile, and I would sing to the Lord between stops.

Following Jesus in this little car was pure joy and a daily exciting adventure!

PRAYER: Thank You, Lord, for Your presence and promise that if we will "go" for You that "You will be with us to the end of the world!" (Matt. 28:19,20)

31
CHRISTMAS TREES IN AFRICA ?

Read Matt. 1:18-25: And she shall bring forth a son, and thou shalt call his name JESUS: for he shall save his people from their sins. (vs. 21)

It was a challenge as Christmas Day drew nearer, to know just how to decorate for the big Christmas program to be held in the Chapel or even how to bring the Christmas atmosphere to our home. We hadn't brought anything like that with us.

On a trip to a town for supplies, we found a tiny, artificial tree with colored bulbs that could stand on our fireplace mantle or even on our table as a center piece. Another missionary lent us a string of lights to hang around the mantle. Although this was a far cry from the elaborate trees and decorations we had enjoyed back in Ohio, we were thankful and touched to have anything at all. The simplicity did not detract from the purpose or warmth of the season. CHRISTMAS WAS HERE!

A look around at the poinsettia trees, lilac-colored Jack-O-Randa, the many blooming golden, red, and purple bushes and flowers everywhere was a gorgeous sight, but there was nothing at all resembling evergreen to be found for a tree or decorations for the Chapel.

Determined to help me find *something* that wouldn't die quickly, Nomsa and Thabsile, armed with their bolo knives (huge bush knives used to cut through tough, thick weeds and bushes), took me on a trek up the mountainside. It was difficult for me to even explain to them what pine needles were like, but finally, after hours of searching, they led us to a grove of very skinny, puny trees faintly similar to evergreens. They cut FOUR of them down and we tied them together to make ONE TREE about five feet tall and reasonably round. I was jubilant! More decorations were gathered from the other missionaries and the tree was installed in the

Chapel, as well as poinsettia flowers and green branches tied with red ribbon. WE WERE READY!

That evening was graduation (called matriculation) for the senior students and a Christmas program was held in the assembly hall. Dave and I were invited. One of the most touching things we remember was *their* Christmas tree—just an ordinary tree, wilting a little because it wasn't evergreen, but decorated fully with large, brightly colored BALLOONS and strings of homemade streamers. It was a 'BIRTHDAY FOR JESUS TREE' in honor of HIS special holiday!!

Our hearts were moved by the simple beauty of that truth captured by their balloon-covered Christmas tree. It was *perfect* and their African way of celebrating Christ's birth was something we'd never forget!

PRAYER: HAPPY BIRTHDAY, LORD JESUS! Thank You for coming to this earth as a baby who grew up to be a Man and to give Your life, later, to die on a Cross for the people of the world. Amen.

32
CHRISTMAS SUNDAY!

Please read Luke 2:1-14: For unto you is born this day in the city of David a Saviour, which is Christ the Lord. (verse 1)

The film about the Lamb of God had arrived! It was a silent movie but with Siswati written across the bottom explaining the meaning when necessary. The African church leaders and all missionary staff gathered for a very precious time of prayer for the program—for all participants, the film, Jerry's message, and above all for the many visitors we expected. It was the first such outreach for this African church and they, along with all of us, were so excited to see what God was going to do!

Many years before, in order to draw a crowd, gifts were promised and distributed to Africans invited to programs—just small gifts of necessity such as salt, matches, or soap. But we had promised nothing but Jesus (through the film of the "Lamb of God" and then Jerry's message on the Love of God which sent His Son to be born on earth at Christmas). Would people come? After all the days of inviting, and all the preparation and prayer and anticipation, would the church still be empty on Christmas Sunday as it usually was during the students' holiday absence?

It wasn't easy for Swazis to travel. There were no busses on Sundays. But soon people started to arrive! Many families were walking. Cars and trucks came filled far beyond capacity. Soon the Chapel began to fill until the place was PACKED!

Our prayers and hopes were realized that wonderful day as Swazis heard the beautiful Christmas music and eagerly watched the film and listened to the message of Christ's birth and death to save the world.

But most important, we prayed that EACH OF THEM WOULD BE SAVED, PERSONALLY!! God's Spirit helped His message and film to be understood and many people committed their lives to Jesus that Christmas Day! We could only praise God for His Goodness and Love in sending His Son, even as the shepherds and people did so long ago!

PRAYER: Dear Father, we thank You for the birth of Christ and pray that *every* day of *every* year, people will hear and believe and receive Him as their Savior and Lord! Amen.

33
WHAT NOW ?

Behold, I will do a new thing; now it shall spring forth; shall ye not know it? I will even make a way in the wilderness, and rivers in the desert. Isaiah 43:19

There was no doubt that summer was in full bloom although Christmas was only one week passed! The beauty that surrounded us could not stop the letdown feeling as the holiday ended on such a high note! God had done *so much*, but now what? With the Christmas program over, there was no longer a special reason for inviting folks to the mission station. What would their attitude be now and how could we continue to reach out to them?

Apprehensively we set out in the VW again, armed with Siswati tracts that explained the gospel. Praying for God's special leading to individuals or groups that He'd prepared to hear His message, we were thrilled and amazed to find Swazis *still* eager and hungry to hear the Word of God! He did not need a special program to draw interest. People had a great need and HE filled that need!

The VW stopped wherever there was a person to share with. What a blessing we experienced day by day as we shared Jesus Christ with anyone who wanted to listen—individuals, small groups, large groups, along the roadside, at the market places, and bus stops. Jesus met them wherever they were, physically and spiritually!

Daily, people received Him into their hearts and lives to be their Savior and Lord! Each one who responded received Bruce Britten's book "How To Become A Christian And How To Live The Christian Life," as well as a Siswati gospel tract. These enabled them to understand more fully Who Jesus is and what their commitment to Him meant.

God helped us to obtain New Testaments at a reasonable price that we could also give to those who needed them.

So the miracle went on as we followed Jesus, and the days and experiences of sharing the Gospel were unbelievable!

PRAYER: Lord God, even today we pray that You would work miracles in the lives of those who know

You, enabling them to share You with others so that the Joy of Salvation might be spread throughout the world!

34
JOAN THOLE – I

I sought the Lord, and he heard me, and delivered me from all my fears. Psalm 34:4

One day, after sharing at the little school on the mountainside, I set out again to try to find a church I'd been invited to preach in.

There was just the Lord and I as I followed Him that day on treacherous ground, for the roads in that general direction were nearly impassable. It seemed that I would never find this church.

At a river point where I could not cross or even turn around, I saw a lane and pulled into it hoping for a spot to turn around. Although you could not tell from the road, it surprisingly turned out to be a home and coming forward to greet me was a very attractive young coloured woman. Fortunately she spoke English and as I explained to her that I was trying to find a church where I had been invited to preach, she burst into tears and suddenly my arms were around her comforting as best I could as we walked together into her home.

Haltingly, still in tears, she told of her desperate loneliness and need for Christian fellowship. She'd been on her knees crying out to God about it when she heard my car and came outside. My explanation and question about the church I was searching for caused her to believe in her heart that God had literally sent me to her at that very moment! The Christian bond that Joan and I immediately felt between us was close and warm, expectant of what God had in store for us!

She mentioned having tea and clapped her hands. Almost instantly a tall African woman appeared in the doorway and as her eyes met mine she dropped to the floor, face down in a worshipful manner. I jumped forward helping her up as Joan explained that she was the hired helper and was unaccustomed to white people.

Tea was served while Joan told of the lonely life she lived as an abused and battered wife, forbidden to even leave her property. Although she had several children, they were attending a Christian boarding school where she also had spent her own school years and had found Christ as her Savior at a young age.

Her conversation was often broken by tears and we would kneel together to pray for her husband's salvation, their marriage, and for their tragic family situation.

A peaceful calmness began to quiet her heart and we rejoiced over our new and unexpected God-given friendship!

It was hard to leave her, but promising to come back and to bring her some personal supplies, I drove off thanking the Lord for leading me there. Her suffering was GREAT but it had brought a faith and beauty in HIM that was rare!

Our meetings were beautiful—bringing joy and encouragement to both of us even though it was years before our prayers were answered.

PRAYER: Lord Jesus, encourage some suffering, lonely soul today and give blessed fellowship and peace to trust in You, no matter what!

(continued)

35
JOAN THOLE – II

Read Psalm 57: Be merciful unto me, O God, be merciful unto me: for my soul trusteth in thee: yea, in the shadow of thy wings will I make my refuge, until these calamities be overpast. Psalm 57:1

Joan and I were eventually separated by an ocean for three years while sporadic letters revealed her increased suffering! My heart would suffer with hers and our prayers would mingle unlimited by distance.

Eventually God led Dave and me back to serve Him again in Swaziland and this time we followed Him to the northern district.

Unexpectedly, one day it was possible to drive south to Joan's home. She flew out of the door rejoicing and excited to see me again! But her smile was *toothless* now and her life was under threat of death by her husband.

She told of her terrible despondence and of crying out to God asking that He send me back to Swaziland to see her again. Praying it repeatedly, she said God comforted her one particular day with the definite impression that *I was on my way!* With lifted spirit and faith, she kept watching for me, and now God had brought us together again!

It was a wonderful reunion but her circumstances were worse. We prayed together as trustingly as we could, thanking God for the *bad* as well as the *good* brought during our separation—most of all praising Him because we loved and trusted Him!

Claiming many glorious promises again for her husband, marriage, and family, we parted again with great expectancy for the future!

PRAYER: Lord Jesus, don't ever let us give up! Lift our hearts to hope in You, our great and loving God!

(continued)

36
JOAN THOLE – III

If thou, Lord, shouldest mark iniquities, O Lord, who shall stand? But there is forgiveness with thee, that thou mayest be feared. Psalm 130:3,4

Many prayers were offered but several long, full years passed before Joan and I could meet again. Dave and I prayed, then drove to her home wondering what we would find.

As we reached the house, several men were working on an auto. One came toward us smiling just as Joan ran toward us. The two met side by side and a *radiant, happy* Joan introduced her husband!

God, in His wondrous way, had answered prayer and transformed this man's life! George, who found Christ as his Savior and Lord, had asked forgiveness of his wife and children for the years of adulterous, violent living he had inflicted. He has since restored his family to love and security based on the Rock foundation of Jesus Christ!

It was beautiful to see and hear of his complete transformation! Joan's face and testimony reflected the praise and adoration she had for God's goodness, mercy, and grace in their lives!

Their aim *together* now is to follow the Lord, to live for His glory, and to point others to Him!

PRAYER: Father, thank You for such an abundant answer to many years of prayer! Please touch other lives and marriages TODAY with Your Salvation and healing. Transform misery and violence into love and beauty that will honor and glorify You!

37
DRUMS IN THE NIGHT

Read: I Kings 17:1-7 and 18:41-46: And it came to pass in the meanwhile, that the heaven was black with clouds and wind, and there was a great rain . . . (18:45)

Summer nights in Swaziland were usually very warm with trillions of stars and loud tropical sounds of crickets, frogs, and night creatures that sang us to sleep.

In the middle of one night, I awoke with a gasp to the startling sound of a distant, steady drum beat—over and over, never changing, never stopping! The drums beat on and on!

Bolting upright in bed with the covers clutched around me, the fearful thought that "THIS IS AFRICA and something's WRONG" speeded into my mind! Soon, Dave too was awake and we wondered together, "WHAT'S happening?"

As the drums continued, we went to the Lord in prayer, then settled down again unable to do anything at that hour except wait and trust in the Lord!

Sleep finally overcame our apprehension but we woke again at daylight still hearing the steady beat of the drums.

Morning brought a hum on the mission station as all of the missionary families pondered the meaning of the drums. In the past, it had sometimes meant a tribal war was taking place. More prayers were offered. Then work on the station was resumed as usual. We would all just have to wait as we followed the Lord that day and see what would happen!

As the African missionaries and friends began to arrive for work, our apprehension was calmed. They explained that the drums were sounding out *prayers from witch doctors* calling for rain! Swaziland was suffering a devastating drought at that time and *our* prayer meetings also were filled with concerned requests for rain. Although the reason for the drums was far better than a tribal war, it was nevertheless eerie to hear the continuing beat from these witch doctors.

Day and night, for weeks, the drums beat on never ending. It was nerve racking and yet, perhaps a constant reminder for all of us to send up prayers to our LIVING LORD to bring nourishing rain on this parched land.

We watched, almost as Elijah had, for the thunder clouds. Finally, thankfully, they CAME bringing an *abundance* of rain!

God's faithfulness and mercy was tremendous and many prayers of thanks and praise were offered.

It was certain that the witch doctors thought *their* prayers had brought the rain. But, mercifully, the drum beats came to a halt!

PRAYER: Thank You, Lord, that YOU are *real* and *alive* and that You hear and answer Your children's prayers without requiring us to paint our bodies or pound on drums to get Your attention! You hear even our whispers and sighs of distress. Thank You for Your goodness and mercy in times of great need! Amen.

38
TRACTS – I

Heaven and earth shall pass away, but my words shall not pass away. Matt. 24:35

At times, Dave needed to find parts or supplies for his work that required us to travel a distance. This was always an adventuresome challenge on the narrow, mountainous roads.

It was during these travels when we saw that hundreds of people walked along the roads alone and in large or small groups.

Bus stops and market places were also crowded along the way. On these trips we never had an interpreter with us, yet we felt *compelled* to share the Gospel of Jesus Christ. Our hearts went out to these folks! It was difficult to pass them by wondering if they'd ever hear of Jesus.

We found ourselves stopping often to share but it was impossible to reach out to all of the people we'd see on these two and a half hour trips.

After a couple of times like this, we began to pray that our God (who can do *anything*) would somehow help us to be able to share Jesus with these Swazis along the roads. Of course, the idea came immediately that we should have tracts in *their* languages (Zulu and Siswati) to distribute freely! But where would we find them and how could we afford the thousands that would be needed?

SOON, after praying more (on just about the third trip to a city), we discovered that a little Christian book store in that place had just the tracts we needed! They were written plainly for the African culture in their languages. Best of all, they were extremely inexpensive at three for one cent! Thrilled at God's wonderful answer to our prayers, we purchased one thousand that very first day!

Excitedly, as we drove home, we stopped over and over on the roads to pass out tracts to the hundreds of people walking or waiting along the way. Literature is scarce in Swaziland so the Swazis are eager to read anything they can get. They read it over and over and then pass it along to family members or friends. If they can't read, then someone else will read it to them. Literature is read until it falls apart! We were sure God would bless these tracts in countless ways!

It was so GREAT to finally have the Gospel to give out and yet, it was still impossible to stop that often to pass out tracts to so many people. By the time we reached home, it was obvious that we would not be able to handle this in that way. But we didn't give up!

Thanking God for His provision and for this new opportunity of reaching many Swazis, we asked the Lord to show us a more effective way to distribute the tracts.

The answer was simple and the trips ahead were a glorious experience of not only following Him but of traveling *with* the Lord, watching HIM put the tracts into the hands of Swazi people whose hearts we believe He had prepared for HIS MESSAGE!

PRAYER: Thank You, Lord, that You cared about everyone on those Swaziland roads at that time! Thank You that You STILL care about people on the roads of life today. May Your mercy and grace reach out to the lost in creative and effective ways even now!

(continued)

39
TRACTS – II

For the word of God is quick, and powerful, and sharper than any two- edged sword, piercing even to the dividing asunder of soul and spirit, and of the joints and marrow, and is a discerner of the thoughts and intents of the heart. Hebrews 4:12

The next trip found us expectant, yet wondering how the Lord would lead.

Praying that we'd be able to give the gospel to as many people as possible between our home and our destination city, we set out armed with hundreds of Zulu and Siswati tracts!

As always, we found hundreds and hundreds of Africans on the roads. As we slowly approached the first group, Dave touched the hooter (horn) lightly while I thrust my hand out the window with a stack of tracts letting loose of them just as we passed by. A gentle wind blew scattering them amongst the crowd and I turned to watch *every* person stoop to pick up a tract! We praised the Lord and again asked His continued help to get His message into the hands of folks whose hearts were open and prepared to understand and to respond to Him.

Claiming God's promises in Hebrews 4:12 and Isaiah 55:ll, we KNEW HE would make this, His Word, "quick and powerful" and it would "not return void but would accomplish His purpose."

What a joyful adventure it was to see our creative Lord get these gospel tracts *directly* to the people as we drove along and to look back to see them opening and reading God's *Living Word!*

PRAYER: Oh Lord, there is absolutely NOTHING too hard for You! What a joy it is to follow Your creative ways and ideas to spread Your gospel message! May Your special guidance bring many to Christ *today!*

(continued)

40
TRACTS – III

So shall my word be that goeth forth out of my mouth; it shall not return unto me void, but it shall accomplish that which I please, and shall prosper in the thing whereto I sent it. Isaiah 55:11

God encouraged us in so many ways, at that time proving that He was not off somewhere in space, but was with us PERSONALLY, literally, guiding these tracts to the people.

There were the countless times that tracts were picked up by large groups delighted to get them even from strangers driving by.

Then there were those walking alone who saw a

pamphlet fly from the car window and we watched as the wind blew it *directly* to them!

Our prayer as I threw them out the window was that the Lord would not let any go to waste but that all would be received and read, resulting in many souls finding Christ!

It was so exciting to see the LORD deliver these gospel tracts. As we approached a lone man sitting on a bank beside the road one morning, his appearance seemed dejected. As we passed by sending out a tract, it stopped in the road at the foot of the bank directly in front of him. But he looked down the bank at it and *didn't move*. By now, my head was out the window watching as I called out to the Lord. By the grace of God, the wind then gently blew the tract straight up the bank and into the man's lap. He opened it and began to READ. Praise God for His loving mercy and care for even one man!

Once a bicyclist wouldn't slow down to receive a pamphlet. Again, I spoke to the Lord as it flew from the window. Amazingly, the wind took it right to the bike and stuck it to the spokes of his front wheel. The man reached forward and peeled it off as he pedaled, putting it into his pocket!

PRAYER: Oh God, how incredibly adequate You are for each and every situation! May we never forget that. Amen.

41
TRACTS – IV

Read Acts 8:26-40: Then Philip opened his mouth, and began at the same scripture, and preached unto him Jesus. (verse 35)

Praying constantly for the nearly 3,000 tracts that we were distributing monthly brought us to often wonder just what results the Lord was bringing from this ministry.

One day as Dave was walking on the station, he saw a student sitting dejectedly against a building trying to read something. Dave stopped to speak to him and saw that it was one of *our* tracts he had. Dave sat down beside the boy asking if he understood what those scriptures meant. His answer was negative so Dave began to explain, verse by verse, the meaning of the gospel from the pamphlet.

This chap asked questions, then slowly his face lit up with understanding. How *thrilled* he was to hear of such a wonderful Savior and how happy he was to be able to commit his life to the Lord Jesus Christ! Afterward he bounced off, no longer sad or depressed. As usual, when Jesus comes into a life, He lifts the spirit and brings new peace and joy to the heart!

How encouraged we were to discover that this boy had received the tract while walking along the road the day before when we were distributing them. Our name was on the back of it!

PRAYER: Lord, we were so happy to know that not only this boy could be saved, but that You were using this means to reach *many* for Jesus Christ! TODAY we pray for special blessing and guidance as You use tracts to spread Your Word! Amen.

42
TRACTS – V

Read Psalm 105:1-5: O give thanks unto the Lord; call upon his name: make known his deeds among the people. Seek the Lord and his strength: seek his face evermore. (verses 1 and 4)

Parts for cars or appliances and things of that sort are usually very hard to get in Swaziland. That's why we were so impressed when the service manager in a repair shop said that our car (which needed a major part for the motor) would be repaired in three days.

That was SUPER!

But, a month later, the VW was still NOT fixed, and it actually took *six weeks!*

Well, in the meantime, what do you do for transportation? For a while we just stayed on the station and I walked to the clinic, post office and butchery to share the Gospel as best I could. It didn't take long until I felt the need to spread my wings. That was when I thought of Dave's motor scooter. It was fairly large, getting him around on the station quickly since the workers were scattered all over the station compound. It seemed like the answer to our need for transportation.

There were two problems to that idea. One was that the mountainous roads were too rocky, rutty, and dust slippery for Dave to agree to let me drive it. Secondly, I would have to wear a skirt and couldn't drive riding side-saddle. (In Swaziland, ladies slacks are absolutely *forbidden.*)

It took a while to convince Dave that I could ride side-saddle behind him without throwing the motor scooter off balance on those treacherous roads. Finally, he agreed and we set off with tracts and Bibles in the front basket. What a ride THAT turned out to be! But surprisingly, zooming around on a thing like that drew young people to us wherever we went, especially young *men!* Our message was heard by a whole *different* group and many of them became Christians during that time!

PRAYER: How thankful we are, Lord, that YOU never run out of creative ways to reach those whom You've prepared to receive Your Son! Help us to keep praying for people to come to Christ and to let *You* lead the way. Amen.

43
OUR INCREASING FAMILY

All scripture is given by inspiration of God, and is profitable for doctrine, for reproof, for correction, for instruction in righteousness. II Timothy 3:16

A new challenge came to us as Bruce Britten introduced ten high school girls who had just rededicated their lives to the Lord during a youth meeting held at the school.

It seemed that these girls had been somewhat irresponsible before this change of heart but now, they sincerely wanted to 'grow' spiritually.

We were happy at the prospect of discipling them and invited them to meet weekly at our home.

The girls came faithfully, together as a class, studying and trying to learn all they could. It was a blessing that kept us on our toes. A close relationship developed as we saw the girls begin to settle down and get serious about their relationship with the Lord.

We would usually have tea and refreshments after their class and sometimes I'd fix a home-cooked meal for them. They began to call us "mum" and "baba".

It was so interesting to learn about their families and home life. This close exposure to their culture was good for us. We enjoyed the girls immensely!

One evening they left particularly late. It was just getting dark so Dave decided to walk them to their dormitory.

As they all stepped out on our lawn, thousands of large, transparent-winged termites were coming up out of the ground. The girls were delighted to see the annual arrival of these *delicacies* and began to run around catching them and actually eating them on the spot.

Of course, Dave was more than shocked at this sight but it wasn't long until they wanted him to try one. He caught one and tried to get up the courage to eat it but just couldn't do it.

THAT delicacy was NOT for him!

The girls appreciated his willingness to try which was more than I could've done!

PRAYER: Father, we thank You for the way You draw people together with Your love that encompasses all peoples and all cultures! Amen.

44
THE JUNIOR CHURCH

Let no man despise thy youth; but be thou an example of the believers, in word, in conversation, in charity, in spirit, in faith, in purity. Till I come, give attendance to reading, to exhortation, to doctrine. I Timothy 4:12,13

It was such a blessing every week to teach these young women, to fellowship together, and to know that God was giving them a desire to serve Him. We were so delighted with them!

Strangely enough, the Lord had a plan to test their eagerness to serve.

Even though the services were not always bilingual, every Sunday Dave and I looked forward to attending the African Evangelical Church that was on the mission station. All of the students were there and a good number of people from the surrounding area attended. The church was fairly large and we began to notice the MANY small children who were usually sent to the balcony to sit and watch quietly. Young African children do not misbehave or disrupt but it was obvious by their faces and general demeanor that they were completely lost in their understanding of the services. Many fell asleep during the sermon. As the Lord began to open our eyes to this, He also helped us to realize that these children needed to be taught while their parents were worshiping.

After praying about the situation for a while, we had opportunity to ask the African pastor, Reverend Gamedze, about children's classes. Of course, he agreed. But the problem was that there was no one willing to teach the children or space in the church for classes.

Many more prayers were lifted up. Then finally one day, the idea came that the group of young women who met with us who were 'growing' and wanting to serve the Lord could, perhaps, be the very 'teachers' we were praying for. We spoke to the pastor and the headmaster, Mr. Harpool, and found them agreeable if Mr. Hutchison and I would teach the girls the lesson first each week, then they would share that lesson with the children! We were thrilled and so were the girls! It was decided to use the assembly hall to split up the children into age groups. The girls would 'pair up' by twos so there would be five classes.

The African parents were delighted to know that their children would be taught the Word of God!

The Lord helped us all to prepare and the time came to begin!

The girls were so excited! The makeshift classrooms were ready and the girls waited in the road to direct children to their new classrooms.

One of the first to appear with his young Swazi parents, walking to the church, was a little boy about three years old dressed only in a beaded string around his waist. Dave and I, watching from a sideline, were thrilled to see him take the hand of one of our young teachers and go to the classroom. In all, thirty-six children attended that day from two years old and up. The children were so happy and eager to learn together!

God's blessings were many on the children and their teachers from that time on. As the girls graduated (matriculated), others would take their places and the Junior Church became a constant part of that African church and a ministry for the students!

PRAYER: Father, we thank You for the way You can open our eyes to the needs around us and for the amazing ways that You work out those needs. Today, Father, work out ways that more children in the world might hear Your Word in an understandable way so they can come to know You! Thank You for Your loving kindness toward children!

45
ANGELIC REBELS – I

If we confess our sins, He is faithful and just to forgive us our sins, and to cleanse us from all unrighteousness. I John 1:9

The Junior Church was thriving and growing in numbers every week until there were finally about sixty children meeting faithfully on Sundays. We kept praising the Lord for His goodness!

One week I was asked by a missionary school teacher if I would teach a Sunday school class of high school girls on a weekly basis. I prayed about it and felt that I should at least try.

After much prayer and study, the day came to begin this new class. It only took the first day to discover that this group was a rebellious, mischievous bunch not interested in learning anything about God or His Word.

How discouraging and disheartening it was weekly to see their apathy toward the Bible and rudeness and even rowdiness during class.

I shuddered at what I had gotten myself into! It brought new respect to my heart for the army of successful Sunday School teachers around the world. Lord bless them all!!

After trying many ways of studying God's word together with them, I was at wit's end one morning to hold their attention. *Suddenly* I stopped in the middle of the lesson and called for a conversational prayer time!

Startled into having to talk to GOD personally, and aloud, the first two girls offered timid, brief sentences. Encouraged that they were responding at all, my heart leaped when the next young lady began asking God's forgiveness for the group's rebellious disrespect for His Word! *The Holy Spirit began to work and many prayers of confession* followed. Soon there were tears and heartfelt prayers for each other! As the class time ended, there was a new feeling of closeness to the Lord and to one another. They asked if we could pray during class next Sunday *again* and I agreed, thankful for such a request from this group.

PRAYER: Father, Your forgiveness is so powerful in touching and changing hearts. We thank You for your love and patience that draws us to Yourself. Amen.

46
ANGELIC REBELS – II

Call unto me, and I will answer thee, and shew thee great and mighty things, which thou knowest not. Jeremiah 33:3

The following week they came into class pleasantly and eagerly, asking to pray for their fellow students. THAT was an answer to much prayer lifted for them during the week and we wasted no time getting started!

It was touching to hear their concerned prayers for friends and classmates! I had brought a Swaziland map and before long we were praying for their towns and families with a finger right on the spot. This progressed to the world map where each girl picked a country or continent to pray for while touching it.

By the time class ended that day, the *world* had prayerfully been *evangelized*.

This was the last Sunday before a long school holiday and we parted reluctantly, thankful for what God was doing for the class.

When the holiday was over, it took a while before we all discovered that *many* Franson students and some of their family members had found Christ during the holiday period. The girls were humbled and grateful to realize how wonderfully God had answered their prayers!

As the girls returned to studying, they helped with different ways to keep God's word challenging. He worked encouragingly in ALL of our lives!

PRAYER: Lord, thank You for Your understanding of rebellious youngsters! Continue to challenge and work through Your Holy Spirit in classes equally or even more rebellious than this one and may they eventually become faithful, loving servants of Yours, who will glorify You in a LASTING way!

47

GOD'S SPIRIT AT WORK IN WINTER

...Not by might, nor by power, but by my spirit, saith the Lord of hosts. Zechariah 4:6

Southern Africa does have a short winter season (June, July, and August) during which time the weather is cool, damp, and MUDDY. There is a very thin layer of ice on puddles at times, but it doesn't freeze solid and doesn't snow.

During that period we found it extremely difficult to witness to folks on the roads or in the open markets or at bus stops as had become our custom. The Swazis were too cold to stand still to talk even with an interpreter.

However, they were still extremely interested to receive gospel tracts. They also were always glad to hear a message at the clinic while waiting for treatment. The response continued to be good. There was a constant moving of God's Spirit in that place all year around.

As the street witnessing diminished because of bad weather, the Lord began to open new doors and opportunities. Dave and I were invited to schools to share the gospel in large assembly meetings. And churches invited Dave to preach. It was exciting and challenging because, if you remember, Dave was a welder and I a homemaker. Neither of us considered ourselves speakers and Dave was not a preacher. But

Dave finds God doing a new thing
enabling him the joy of preaching.

GOD, in answer to prayer, would give us HIS message to fit the opportunity He had brought. It was 'stretching' and fulfilling to follow Him in this way! There were always folks who needed and wanted to receive Jesus Christ as their Savior and Lord. It was thrilling to know that the Holy Spirit was NOT hibernating during the winter season!

PRAYER: Lord, it's so good that You never sleep nor slumber but Your Spirit *always* works to find and to save people who will seek You! Today may Your Spirit convict and win souls around the world and also in America. People need You, Lord, in ALL seasons, spring, summer, fall, and winter! Thank You, Lord! Amen.

48
"JUST AS I AM"

For whosoever shall call upon the name of the Lord shall be saved. Romans 10:13

Witnessing at homes became more and more of a delight as the Lord began to lead in that way.

The Swazis were friendly and receptive to us and to God's word in such a way that it was evident that the Holy Spirit was still preparing the way!

Nomsa and I would pray and follow the Lord in whatever direction He led, sometimes sharing and visiting in four or five homes in one day. Folks were always interested to hear about the Lord Jesus and to have questions answered. Many families eagerly received Jesus into their lives together on these visits. It was encouraging to see each day where the Lord would lead us and how He would make the way to share the gospel in a saving way ALWAYS meeting people 'where they were' in their lives and always in a different way. The song, "Just As I Am," became so apparently true!

Time after time, He lifted people in despair, heartache, suffering and loneliness, and brought hope, peace, and love to broken lives. How exciting it was! How exciting it STILL is to KNOW that Jesus is doing the same today!

He will meet YOU where YOU are and bring new life to YOU also, if you'll let Him!

Friend, if there's any doubt at all in your mind that you have ever committed your life to Jesus, won't you please do it now?

Just pray this prayer from your heart:

Dear Father, thank You for sending Jesus to die on the cross for *my* sins. Forgive me, Father, for every sin that's ever been in my life. Lord Jesus, come into my heart to be my Savior and Lord forever! Help me to live for You. Thank You for saving my soul. In Jesus name I pray. Amen.

Jesus *will* answer your prayer and come into your life and will bring you the hope and peace and love that He's brought to many, many others! God bless you!!

49
THE DOG ENCOUNTER

Read Psalm 91:9-12: For he shall give his angels charge over thee, to keep thee in all thy ways. They shall bear thee up in their hands, lest thou dash thy foot against a stone. (verses 11,12)

As spring began to bloom again, it seemed that Swaziland was just humming with people coming and going. The burden to share the saving power of Jesus Christ with them sent me out again daily as God led me to those He'd prepared to hear.

One day a request to make a sick call took Nomsa and I up the side of a mountain toward a humble kraal (Swazi mud-walled, thatched roof home).

Suddenly, out of nowhere, came a fierce, barking dog attacking us from behind! Before we could do anything, he was biting the calf of my right leg!

I screamed and flung my leg so hard the dog fell loose. Then Nomsa kept him back with a stick for what seemed an eternity until we heard a man shouting. The dog slinked away at his master's voice.

Fortunately, the Lord had protected in His unusual way. My leg was bleeding and bruised, but not as badly as it could have been! Instead of turning back down the mountain to the car, we proceeded on toward the man standing in the doorway who appeared obviously ill.

What a blessing was in store for us as we visited with this stranger who was very ill, but who knew the Lord in a close, personal way. The bond of Christ made us feel like old friends.

It was heartwarming to fellowship together and pray for this child of God.

As we descended the mountain carefully, watching for the dog, we were thankful that the Lord had given courage to follow through on that visit when our inclination was to run away as fast as possible.

Neither Nomsa nor I would ever forget that fearful, but rewarding episode! My leg was painful but NOT seriously injured!

PRAYER: Lord, following You teaches us so much! Please keep us close so that we might not miss even one single experience that You have planned for us! Amen.

50

THE TREES

Matt. 19:13-15: Then were there brought unto him little children that he should put His hands on them, and pray: and the disciples rebuked them. But Jesus said, "Suffer little children and forbid them not, to come unto me: for of such is the kingdom of heaven." (verses 13,14)

A family had found Jesus in their home one morning. Nomsa and I had shared at a market place and then along the roadside, before spotting this home on the side of a mountain. We had climbed up in the sunlight finding several members of this family responsive to receive the Lord Jesus Christ into their lives!

Nomsa and I were gratefully climbing back down the mountain when we heard voices and laughter. Stopping to look around, we saw nothing. Yet voices and laughter continued with nobody in sight. Finally we looked UP and in the trees above us were several young children chattering and *hanging over our heads!*

Nomsa spoke to them in her friendly, loving way and soon they were perched on their branches listening intently as we told them of the love that Jesus has for children.

Looking up into the trees as they clung to the branches, these kids were like happy little monkeys. But praise the Lord, they were NOT little monkeys but African children that God had created to love and belong to Himself. It was a thrilling moment when their questions were answered and these delightful children wanted Jesus in their lives! Bowing their heads and hearts while still in the trees, they prayed and asked Him into their lives!

The Bible says there is great joy in Heaven when even *one* person receives Jesus and Nomsa and I also felt a great joy that morning as these children surrendered their lives to Christ. He met them in the trees.

There's a lovely poem and song about a tree, but THIS tree holding African children became the most outstanding tree in our memory!

PRAYER: Thank You, Jesus, that You care for children and can meet them even in a TREE to give them the most precious gift of all time, the gift of ETERNAL LIFE! Amen.

51

FEARLESSNESS

Read Romans 10:14-16 and vs. 17: How then shall they call on him in whom they have not believed? and how shall they believe in him of whom they have not heard? and how shall they hear without a preacher? (verse 14)

Bumping along in the little VW alone one day, feeling compelled to share the gospel with whomever the Lord put in my path, it was always delightful to find people open and receptive to the Lord! Two young men not only wanted to receive Jesus but had many questions and asked if they could ride along with me for a while so we could talk. They piled into the back seat and soon became 'helpers' as we'd stop to talk to others along the road. They were contagious with their joy in Christ and eagerly shared their newly-found faith. Soon there were two more 'brand new' Christian young men in the VW who needed a ride and we merrily chatted and sang as God led us along.

Swaziland was really primitive, so it was a real surprise to me when I saw a *bulldozer* moving dirt on a bank by the side of the road ahead of us.

My amazement slowed me down to a stop right beside it. Curiosity in what I was doing stopped the driver of the 'dozer also and, unbelievably I stepped right out of the car onto the bank and another step put me directly *onto* the bulldozer.

There were three men on it who, seeing the Bible in my hand, removed their hats and greeted me in English. I briefly shared the Gospel as they nodded in agreement. These men were already Christians! They asked me to pray for them and then I quickly stepped back down into the VW again. This experience caused me to realize God's unusual protection and supernatural help in not only keeping me safe, but in putting me *where He wanted me.*

He took away all fear and most of the time I felt as though I was someone *else* watching this lady speak to people about the Lord and OFTEN in most unusual places or circumstances!

PRAYER: Dear Lord, You overcame all fear and circumstances in order to get Your gospel out! Spread Your word TODAY by the power of Your Holy Spirit! Amen.

52
BURIAL MOUNTAIN

Read I Corinthians 15:1-8: For I delivered unto you first of all that which I also received, how that Christ died for our sins according to the scriptures; and that he was buried, and that he rose again the third day according to the scriptures. (verses 3,4)

One mountain that was in view from our home on the mission station was a distinct cone shape with GREEN trees all year around. In Swaziland that was unusual because there were very few evergreens.

We soon were told that it was a "burial" mountain for chiefs and was guarded day and night from intruders. White people were not to set foot on it we were informed. This mountain seemed impressive and mysterious!

Then came the death of the local chief (equivalent to a mayor in America). The Swazis mourned respectfully, although they considered him to be a heavy drinker (home brew) for many years.

Out of love and compassion for the Swazi people, Dave and I wanted to go to the funeral if it would not be an intrusion. Our Swazi friends seemed glad and invited us not only to come, but they came to our home to take us, personally, themselves. We felt humbled by the mutual love and bond between us. The funeral was to be held at the chief's *kraal* at the foot of Burial Mountain.

Our hearts were touched upon arrival by the great number of mourners.

Hundreds of women were sitting on the ground while the men stood or sat in a separate area.

Chairs were brought for Dave and me, but I went, instead, to the women and sat among them on the ground. They moved closer and shared a mat with me. Dave was asked to speak at the funeral.

It was thrilling to find that Christ was being honored and shared with the crowd. People were crying—not because of this death, but for repentance of the sin in their lives. The Spirit of God was moving in a mighty way that day.

As time came to carry the body up onto the burial mountain, Dave and I prepared to leave. But our Swazi friends took our hands and led us along with them. It was an honor to be among the few white folk ever allowed to set foot on that mountain.

The chief's body was lifted and wrapped in a soft animal skin, then carried by six young Swazi warriors dressed in their traditional warrior gear. It was a colorful and touching sight as the mourners sang their Zulu laments traveling up the side of the mountain.

At the burial sight, several men again spoke compellingly of Christ and the Gift of Eternal Salvation through Him as the chief's body was lowered into the grave. Swazis passed by sprinkling a handful of dirt over him and a long line began wending slowly back down the mountain path still singing in their beautiful harmony.

From on down the mountain we suddenly heard screaming. Then slowly, the message passed up through the line that the chief's younger brother had hung himself at the chief's kraal during the burial ceremony.

What a SHOCK it was for the family and friends to find him in that way at that time! It was hard to grasp, but another *funeral* had to be prepared for before the chief's burial was even an hour old. How terribly sad that his loved one had felt so hopeless!

PRAYER: Father, thank You that those who belong to You through having received Christ into their hearts, need NEVER be utterly hopeless! Truly, "death can have no sting and the grave can have no victory," for we shall live eternally in Heaven with YOU someday! Amen. (I Cor. 15:57)

53
MILLION DOLLAR PRAYERS

Call unto me, and I will answer thee, and shew thee great and mighty things, which thou knowest not. Jeremiah 33:3

Mrs. "Q" (as we called her because her name was too difficult to pronounce) came to our home twice weekly to do laundry and floors. An African widow who spoke English, she was raising four small grandchildren and times were difficult for her. We became friends and looked forward to being together.

One morning, her usually happy face was sad with tears gleaming in her eyes. Her answer to my questions was that another drought was ruining crops and the people of Swaziland had less and less to eat. She had been praying as she walked that morning, asking the Lord for rain.

My heart was touched, and suddenly we moved together, climbed up on kitchen stools close by, held hands, and began to pray together. Our hearts were bound as one with our lifted voices, first Mrs. Q's in Siswati. I couldn't understand, but we cried together in agreement. Then my prayer began and I found myself asking God for *immediate* help! In fact, I even asked that AMERICA would send food or money to Swaziland SOON to help in this desperate need! My heart jumped at such a bold request. As far as I knew, America didn't even know of Swaziland's latest drought disaster. Together, we claimed Jeremiah 33:3 and, trusting the Lord to work out His miracle answer in His way, we went on about our day, happily!

Within a week, as I walked to the vegetable stand on the station, I found the latest Swazi newspaper with bold headlines and front page story, "AMERICA SENDS ONE MILLION DOLLARS TO SWAZILAND FOR FOOD." I was so ecstatic, praising the Lord for days until Mrs. Q came again and I could show her the answer to our prayers! Together we thanked God as never before!

Two weeks later, news came again that America had sent MORE financial help. This time it was TWO MILLION DOLLARS!

PRAYER: THANK YOU, LORD, that You *still* can feed the 'five thousand' and even MORE than that from Your resources. HOW GREAT THOU ART! We LOVE YOU and THANK You again! Amen.

54
NO INTERPRETERS – I

Read Exodus 3:9 through 4:14: And the Lord said unto him, Who hath made man's mouth? or who maketh the dumb, or deaf, or the seeing, or the blind? have not I the Lord? Now therefore go, and I will be with thy mouth, and teach thee what thou salt say. (verses 4:ll,12)

Nomsa and Thabsile had matriculated (graduated) and gone away—Nomsa to nursing school and Thabsile to teaching school. We were so proud of them and thankful for all that the Lord had done through them!

Yet I was also restless and sad at times because now there was no interpreter with a real heart to share the gospel and help people find Christ. My prayers became more and more desperate. There was a deep burden to continue to reach the people on the roads and in the market places and bus stops with the message of Christ. What was I to do?

Dawn was breaking one morning as I cried unto the Lord. Then I felt so strongly His urging that I should go out, get into our VW and follow His leading to people. I bolted up from my prostrate position and paced the floor, crying. How could I go anywhere now? It was only dawn—not even breakfast time yet. Where would I go? And, even worse, WHO WOULD INTERPRET FOR ME? I decided that I must be getting this message wrong or that I was misunderstanding what the Lord wanted me to do. I continued in prayer and Bible reading until time to fix breakfast (hours later).

As Dave and I shared coffee later, I tried to explain what happened. I couldn't understand. Yet there was a growing uneasiness about it inside me. We prayed together and asked the Lord for interpreters again.

The uneasiness grew into downright misery as the day went on! I felt terrible pain in my heart that I had deliberately DISOBEYED the Lord! Yet I could not see how I could possibly have carried out His direction to get in our VW, ALONE, at dawn—without an interpreter's help to reach people for Christ? What people at that hour, and how, without help???

PRAYER: Oh God, thank You for Your Holy Spirit's power to guide and to lead. Thank You for His *convicting* power for disobedience or insensitivity to Your leading. Help us TODAY to follow You and trust in You!

(continued)

55
NO INTERPRETERS – II

And the people said unto Joshua, The Lord our God will we serve, and his voice will we obey. Joshua 24:24

By evening I was just miserable with a heavy, convicting sense of having disobeyed God. It was sheer agony!

At bedtime, unable to stand this any longer, I told Dave that the next morning, if I sensed the Lord's leading me out to witness, even at dawn, and without an interpreter, I would have to go because I could not stand another miserable day of disobedience. Having seen my suffering, he understood and prayed for God's guidance and protection over me.

Most of the night I spent in prayer. By dawn I tearfully and prayerfully followed the Lord's guidance into the VW, across the mission compound, bearing right and headed straight up the mountain road into the Swaziland sunrise. I was shocked to see MANY people walking *already!*

Through blinding tears, I saw a dear African sister-in-Christ from the Mission church standing beside the road at her home. She couldn't speak English and I couldn't speak Siswati but I pulled up beside her. Knowing that I usually had an interpreter with me, she motioned quizzically to the empty seat beside me and then toward the road. I lifted my Bible and tracts trying to communicate that, although I was alone, I was *still* going to try to share the gospel, Lord willing. But, I didn't know *how.* She saw my tears and I folded my hands and bowed in prayer, then pointed to her. As I pulled slowly away, she folded her hands and bowed in prayer for me and in the side mirror, I watched her praying until she was out of sight!

Somehow, I BELIEVED that God *was* going to answer her prayers!

PRAYER: Oh God, once again I thank You that *You can overcome* any kind of barrier, even language to communicate Your blessed Word wherever and whenever You choose if we will obey and follow You! Amen.

(continued)

56
NO INTERPRETERS – III

Read Psalm 40:1-10: I delight to do thy will, O my God: yea, thy law is within my heart. (verse 8)

No sooner had Mrs. Xaba slipped from sight in my rear view mirror when I saw an African lady coming toward me dressed in colorful native dress. Rolling the window down, I held out a tract for her. To my surprise, she thanked me in ENGLISH and understood and spoke it plainly! She was headed toward the Mission compound. I offered her a ride and turned the car around heading back to where I'd just come from. My praying friend looked up as we passed by, smiled, and raised a hand thankfully to heaven.

It WAS an answer to prayer as I discovered that God had so prepared the heart of this woman beside me that she quickly questioned, then shared her need for Christ! She had heard the gospel before, but had never committed her life to the Lord. She was so ready that, at her request, I pulled over by the side of the mountain and she prayed to receive Jesus Christ into her heart to be her Savior and Lord! We both were overjoyed and I was so THANKFUL that God had led me to someone that I could communicate to *without an interpreter!* Immediately, she was concerned for her family members without Christ. She said her home was so remote that it could not be reached by car. So I invited her to come to mine. When we reached it, I gave her Siswati tracts and a couple of Bibles so *she* could share God's message with her family. We prayed together for her loved ones and she left for home, singing happily.

My heart leaped! It was *just now time* to fix breakfast and awaken Dave. We rejoiced together as he heard the story of God's *special* guidance at dawn and WITH NO INTERPRETER!

From then on, every morning for six weeks, the Lord led me out at dawn *without* a translator and guided me to people He had prepared to hear His Word. It was thrilling to see the daily response! Sometimes a whole group would receive the Lord. But ALWAYS there was *someone* who would come into the kingdom! Then I would go back home, wake Dave, and fix breakfast by 7:00 A.M.!

PRAYER: Dear God, HOW GREAT THOU ART! We praise you that you are not limited by language barriers and that your timing is always perfect no matter how early or how late! Help us to trust you more and follow you to become "fishers of men" daily! Amen.

57
GOD'S POWER

For I am not ashamed of the gospel of Christ: for it is the power of God unto salvation to every one that believeth: to the Jew first, and also to the Greek. Romans 1:16

After six weeks of witnessing daily at dawn without a translator, the Lord gave me the courage to FOLLOW HIM throughout the days wherever He would lead, *even without interpreters.*

It was such a challenge and blessing to discover daily how unlimited our God is!

One afternoon, I hesitatingly approached a large group of people waiting for a bus. I wanted desperately to share Jesus with them and, strangely enough, I told them so. Immediately, a young man answered in excellent English telling me that he would interpret for me if I wished to speak. Of course, I was overjoyed to see and experience God's provision as together we shared the Gospel of Jesus Christ and saw people surrender their lives to Him unashamedly right there at the bus stop. How faithfully God reaches out with His Gift of Love, mercy, and grace!

The young man begged me to go to a large school nearby to share Jesus Christ with the children. I agreed to do it if he would help by interpreting.

He led us to the school and to the Headmaster but lost his courage to explain why I was there. Trusting in his interpretation, I tried to explain. The Headmaster understood and obligingly invited me to come the next week for a fifteen minute presentation of the Gospel to the whole student body!

The amazing outcome of that visit brings thanksgiving to my heart for our great and loving God!

PRAYER: Father, there is no greater love than Yours. Thank You for spreading it so generously! Amen.

(continued)

58
NGWANA SCHOOL – I

But the Lord said unto me, Say not I am a child: for thou shalt go to all that I shall send thee, and whatsoever I command thee thou shalt speak. Be not afraid of their faces: for I am with thee to deliver thee, saith the Lord. Then the Lord put forth his hand, and touched my mouth. And the Lord said unto me, Behold, I have put my words in thy mouth. Jeremiah 1:7,8,9

The day to go to Ngwana School arrived, very hot and beautiful. As I drove into the school's courtyard I saw the HUGE student body standing almost at attention in a mass facing a long building.

Carrying my flannelgraph lesson and stand past the group, toward their teachers who were situated in front of the students, my heart raced! How could I communicate to such a large group outdoors without a translator or even a microphone?

Then a young man stepped out from among the line of teachers facing the group and with a deep, booming voice (in English) he told me he would be interpreting, and then quickly helped set up the flannelgraph.

The children were various sizes from very small (in front) to high school age. As I looked out over the crowd, the interpreter explained there were seven hundred students and no assembly hall. Therefore, assembly gatherings such as this, had to be held in this courtyard.

About fourteen hundred curious eyes watched my every move as they stood touching shoulders in rows, nearly meeting back to back, as though they were all packed into a huge, invisible box! Standing in the middle of them was the Headmaster! I was so excited and felt the love of God pouring through me for them as Joe, the teacher translator, and I began sharing the Gospel message of Jesus Christ!

The flannelgraph helped explain the virgin birth, some of Christ's life, and then His substitutional death on the cross for our sins.

Joe's voice was *booming* out our message in Siswati. But surprisingly, he had questions which he wanted answered each time BEFORE interpreting! Joe, obviously, had never heard the gospel and seemed almost to forget that we were NOT ALONE!

PRAYER: Father, how exciting it is to follow You and to have the blessing of sharing Your "unspeakable Gift" of Christ in such unique ways and circumstances. Thank You, Amen.

(continued)

59
NGWANA SCHOOL – II

But as many as received him, to them gave he power to become the sons of God, even to them that believe on his name: John 1:12

The Lord had so prepared Joe (the teacher-interpreter at Ngwana School) to *believe* and *receive* His word, that as I shared the Gospel and Joe translated for the seven hundred interested students, he was obviously coming to an understanding and belief in the Lord Jesus Christ even as we spoke to the children. Quickly asking questions while growing more animated with each answer and with the progression of the message of Christ, Joe's enthusiasm was mounting fast.

It seemed incredible that, while sharing Jesus with seven hundred children, the translator, himself, was also being ministered to as if we were having a private conversation. It was such a unique situation.

Just as the message was about to reach its peak, the children began to move toward me. Not with harmful intent, but with excitement and *great enthusiasm!* The whole 'mass' of students moved, eager to touch and feel the flannelgraph "Jesus" figures and me. My heart jumped with happiness at seeing such a large group so eager over the gospel!

The twelve teachers standing behind me realized the danger of my being injured or crushed in the excitement of such a crowd pressing in on me. They quickly moved between the children and myself just as the flannelgraph stand went over. Locking hands together, the teachers were able to keep pushing the children back from me while Joe and I finished the Gospel message!

The Lord led in offering an invitation and I could only praise Him as Joe and all 12 teachers, as well as the Headmaster and about five-hundred of the seven-hundred students, responded in prayer to receive Jesus Christ into their hearts and lives!!

It was tremendous then to have the Headmaster step out of the middle of the crowd to invite me to come back EVERY WEEK to share for fifteen minutes. The Lord opened that way for me to be able to disciple the children as much as possible.

They were usually so eager and excited to hear the message that when the little VW would arrive, it would be so quickly surrounded that I could not even open the door. The children and I became very close in spite of the language barrier. WHAT A BLESSING they were!

PRAYER: Father, even now I thank You for those children and ask You to work in their hearts wherever they may be. Draw them close to You even as You did in those days. Thank You for leading me to them and for the joy and excitement of that experience.

60

NDGUNYA SCHOOL

Behold, I stand at the door, and knock: if any man hear my voice, and open the door, I will come in to him, and will sup with him, and he with me. Revelation 3:20

It was a crisp early morning. The VW moved slowly up the mountain as I prayed for the Lord's leading.

Soon a car was in sight by the side of the road with two men working under the boot (hood).

With a prayerful heart, I stopped, handing each a tract. They spoke English and asked many questions until they had heard the whole gospel message. They were happy to share that they also were Christians but immediately pointed to a field across the road where a group of children sat in the sunshine with their teacher doing lessons.

Nearby was a small school. The men wanted me to ask the principal to let me share the gospel with the children. Before I could answer, the principal came out of the building and walked toward us. The men asked him and he gave permission and then spoke to the teacher.

Soon I found myself sharing the message of Jesus with these cute, young, African children. Their hearts were eager and open and they and their teacher received the Lord Jesus!

An invitation was offered for me to share this message with the entire school the next morning.

What a joy it was to face the one-hundred-twenty smiling children and their teachers, telling them of the love of Christ and His death on the cross for them. Many believed and received Jesus!

Again, I was asked to come back weekly and so had the opportunity to help the entire school to 'grow' in their Christian life!

PRAYER: Father, following You is so exciting as You open such unexpected doors and opportunities and, by Your Spirit, bring souls into Your kingdom. I thank You again for Your great love for children! Extend that love to kids today who need to know Jesus! Amen.

61
TODAY IS THE DAY OF SALVATION

The Lord is . . . not willing that any should perish, but that all should come to repentance. IIPeter 3:9

There were many people on the road as I gave out gospel tracts one sunny afternoon again seeking those whom the Lord had prepared to hear His message.

Finally meeting three young women at a bus stop, I reached out to them with the colorful tracts. They then began asking questions.

Gently and lovingly the Lord guided the answers

until two of them admitted they were Christians. But, the third one was not.

Her friends began telling her of all that Jesus had done for *them*. Tears started to roll down her cheeks. They excitedly shared again, in Siswati, how Jesus had died for her, personally. She shouted out that she needed this Jesus in her life. Her friends and I were thankful and explained the sinner's prayer to commit herself to Christ.

But in all my experiences, for the first and only time, I saw a person who could NOT pray to receive Jesus. She WANTED to. We tried to HELP her, first in English then in Siswati. She sobbed heartbrokenly. Her friends begged her even just to repeat after them. But she simply could not.

My heart flooded with compassion and, for the first and only time also, *I* prayed instead of her for Jesus to come into HER heart.

Only the Lord knows if she was just unable to pray because of her emotion or whether her heart had been hardened by previous rejection of Him as the Bible tells us can happen.

As I left the three with literature and my address so they could write, she was still crying. Her friends were lovingly trying to console and encourage her.

PRAYER: Lord, wherever this young lady is today, we pray that she has prayed, HERSELF, by now to receive You and is living a life that honors You! By Your mercy, reach out to those today who need to be saved. Help people to know that TODAY IS THE DAY OF SALVATION and not to harden their hearts to Your loving call to them. Thank You, Amen.

62
THE THREE DAVIDS

Seeing therefore it remaineth that some must enter therein, and they to whom it was first preached entered not in because of unbelief: Again, he limiteth a certain day, saying in David, Today, after so long a time: as it is said, Today if ye will hear his voice, harden not your hearts. Hebrews 4:6,7

Dave and I had driven to the nearest little town for supplies, but soon found ourselves speaking to people about Christ.

The VW moved slowly, stopping as God led, trusting Him to lead us again to prepared hearts.

In the center of this primitive town we found two striking young Swazi men walking together, laughing, enjoying each other.

Somewhere in their twenties and close in build, one was dressed in the colorful native way. The other wore ordinary slacks and shirt. Both spoke excellent English and each was named David.

My husband, David, began sharing the message of Jesus Christ. The two listened intently. The modern David rejoiced and said he'd been a Christian for quite a while. His friend was full of questions, admitting that he had never received this Jesus into His life.

When his questions ran out, he still was not ready to surrender his life to the Lord, but instead, asked if he could come to our home in a few days for a visit and to hear more. He said he would come and find Jesus at our home.

Dave exhorted the young man even as we returned to the car that "today is the day of salvation" and NOW was the time while the Holy Spirit was knocking on his heart's door (Revelation 3:20) to pray and receive Jesus. But instead, he requested directions, saying he'd be with us in a few days. Dave prayed heartily for both Davids and we drove on sadly.

We never saw him again and can only hope that somehow he followed through and asked Jesus to be his Savior and Lord.

PRAYER: Dear Father, reach out again TODAY, by Your Spirit, to help people who've put off receiving Jesus. Help them to pray and ask your Son into their heart and life. Thank You for Your mercy toward them. Help the two Davids wherever they are right now. For Jesus sake, Amen.

Two African Davids who are friends,
one in Western dress, the other in native dress.

63

THE BOYS' CHOIR

Read Psalm 146:1-5: While I live will I praise the Lord: I will sing praises unto my God while I have any being. (verse 2)

African voices need no instruments but have a unique harmonic blend which we loved to hear! At Franson Christian High School, students were always singing and the sound carried up the mountain to our home. One particular group we often heard was that of young men's voices. Their vibrant songs floated all over the mission station.

One day we followed the sound to the chapel and found ten young men enjoying a practice session of African gospel music!

When they finished, it didn't take long to discover they were *future* ministers who wanted to become disciplemakers. By their request, they started coming weekly to our home to learn more about evangelism and discipling. But always, they would have a little singing practice while with us also. It became a high spot in our week to fellowship and share with these young men and then to enjoy their gospel songs.

They traveled all over Swaziland singing for different occasions and became quite a well-known group.

The Lord used them also to interpret for us. It was a blessing to watch them grow and begin serving Him as opportunities opened!

Today they are ministers, teachers and government leaders in Swaziland who *still*, occasionally, get together to sing for something special!

PRAYER: Lord, what a blessing to look back on that wonderful group and the joy we had together! May You continue to inspire others through them. Make their lives fruitful for Your glory! Amen.

64

THE NOT SO RELAXING PICNIC PLACE

Read Ephesians 6: 10-18: Wherefore take unto you the whole armour of God, that ye may be able to withstand in the evil day, and having done all, to stand. (verse 15)

There were times when it seemed good to have a relaxing afternoon. One sunny day, we planned a picnic to be enjoyed at a beautiful spot on our way to get supplies.

The place in mind was a restful looking hillside overlooking a lovely, but *extremely* rocky valley beside an equally rocky mountain.

Happy for the opportunity to enjoy a light lunch on a blanket while taking in this neat view, we hardly started until we became aware of voices coming toward us. Dave somehow felt a strangeness and hurried out to the road for a 'look see'. Quickly returning, he informed me that, almost unbelievably, a number of unfriendly-looking people were coming from different directions and we needed to move out FAST! Dave has never been an alarmist, so I threw things back in the basket as he grabbed the blanket and we RAN to the car.

A sense of security returned as the motor started and we pulled away.

Yes, the people *did* look different and four men dressed scantily in feathers, skins, and beads chanted and danced in unison as we drove past them.

Later, as we told Mrs. Q (a Swazi friend and helper) of this incident, she startlingly informed us that these men we'd seen were Witch Doctors and that many people had mysteriously disappeared from that area *never* to be seen again. Others had been found dead with parts of their bodies missing. She said she and other Swazi people would never even walk through that section, let alone stop to have a picnic. I confessed that I had driven along that road alone, witnessing at different times.

Mrs. Q's answer is still encouraging as I reminisce. She said, "You can do this and be safe because GOD goes with you!"

PRAYER: Lord, thank You that Your guardian angels often go before and with and after us even when we may not know it. Amen.

65
FISH AND CHIPS

Then Peter opened his mouth, and said, Of a truth I perceive that God is no respecter of persons: But in every nation he that feareth him, and worketh righteousness, is accepted with him. Acts 10:34,35

A certain bus stop where many folks gathered was also the location of a small, very dirty, rough looking building with "Fish And Chips" written across the front. Curiosity drove me to investigate by going inside one morning.

The darkness was overwhelming! The cook and helpers could not speak English, but pointing to a loaf of bread, I paid, handed each of them a tract, tried to smile encouragingly, and walked outside.

One young helper ran after me reaching for tracts. Immediately turning toward the crowd milling around, he began speaking Siswati while passing the tracts among the people and gaining their attention!

Countless times later, I returned to that place. Always he would come out and, together, we would distribute the Good News—he speaking in his soft Siswati, and I sharing in English with those who could understand.

He was obviously blind in one eye, very ragged and unkempt, yet a glow from his love for Christ shone on his face proving again that "you can't judge a book by its cover."

Although we could not converse, we shared a sense of joy together knowing that people were reading and hearing of Christ, the living, loving SAVIOR!

PRAYER: Lord, you're the One who looks on the heart and NOT on appearance! Encourage some shy, poor person today and use their inadequacies for Your glory and honor! Thank You, Lord Jesus! Amen.

66
THE WORKERS AND THE GOSPEL

And this is the record, that God hath given to us eternal life, and this life is in his Son. He that hath the Son hath life; and he that hath not the Son of God hath not life. IJohn 5:11,12

Mornings were a delight at Mhlosheni! Everything was shimmering with a misty freshness. There was always a fragrance of blooming flowers or trees. It was the kind of quiet beauty that brought a feeling within that THIS DAY WAS GOOD, and that something GOOD would happen!

Dave started each work day by sharing the Word of God with the workers on the station. The English-speaking cook would interpret and the workers were attentive. This became a highlight for Dave and a fitting way to start each beautiful day.

We prayed much for these people and as the first Christmas approached, we planned a time of sharing the birth of Christ and the whole Gospel message, using interpreters and flannelgraph.

Dave and I were so excited and expectant as the day arrived!

God was with us and had surely prepared the hearts of these men, women, and children workers through the daily messages they had been hearing from His Word.

At that time, there were forty workers. All of them came to this special Christmas sharing. As Dave told of Christ's birth, he also shared His life, death, burial and resurrection.

Tears streamed down some faces, others listened with mouths open, and some just frowned trying to grasp the meaning.

But as Dave finished and invited them to believe in and receive Jesus as THEIR Savior and Lord, PERSONALLY., eighteen of the forty attending committed their hearts and lives to Christ!

PRAYER: Dear God, remembering Your loving touch upon hearts that are open and receptive causes us to pray again, that *today* people would believe and receive Jesus into their hears as their PERSONAL Savior and Lord!! Amen.

67
SNAKES AND THE STILL, SMALL VOICE

Read Psalm 121: He will not suffer thy foot to be moved: he that keepeth thee will not slumber. (verse 3)

Thinking of Africa automatically brings mental pictures of jungle, wild animals, snakes, and such.

Although much of Africa is jungle-covered, southern Africa is NOT. Monkeys, kudu, springbok, dyker and such are fairly numerous but lions, tigers, elephants, giraffes, etc. are mostly found on game preserves.

Snakes, however, ARE plentiful and many deadly and poisonous species can be found there.

During the South African mild 'winter' season it's rare to even see a snake. However, one dark, wet night, as I prepared with torch (flashlight) and slicker to visit and encourage an ill missionary friend, a thought came clearly into my mind—"watch out for snakes." After the clearly into my mind—"watch out for snakes." After the third time, I almost answered aloud, "But we haven't seen a snake in quite a while."

Nevertheless, since my feeling for snakes is comparable to spiders, I went really cautiously, shining the torch all around ahead of me. Not a glimpse of a snake! Well, maybe on my return . . . but after ministering to my friend, I walked home watching very carefully without a sign of a snake! It was late and I hurried to bed wondering about the inner warning that now seemed unnecessary. Why????

Early the next morning, I scurried to discover what all the shouting I heard was about. An African worker had nearly stepped on a big black mamba which is *very deadly!* Later, there was another flurry over a snake and before the morning was over, three snakes had been killed. One (a cobra) was very close to the path I had traveled the night before! I remembered the inner warning with a THANKFUL HEART.

PRAYER: Oh Lord, help us to always heed Your inner warnings as we head for trouble in our life. Thank You. Amen.

68
DAVE AND THE COBRA

Read Psalm 141: Lord, I cry unto thee: make haste unto me; give ear unto my voice when I cry unto thee. (verse 1)

Dave and I were enjoying the memorizing of God's Word and began to compete, making it fun and challenging.

Since he was busy all over the station, and I had various tasks, we would see each other throughout the day.

Immediately, we'd challenge the other to quote our verse for that day, word and reference perfect.

One particular morning, Dave was learning a verse

as he climbed our mountain to check the mission's gravity water system. Now in Africa, the men carry a stout club for protection (called a nob kerrie). Dave, who is a big man, 6'2", 165 lbs., had found a sturdy 7' staff that he always took when walking, especially on the mountain. But this time his mind was on the Bible verse, forgetting the much-needed staff.

All was O.K. with the water, and coming back down he was reviewing the verse, intending to stop by our house to challenge me.

Suddenly, he was face to face with a huge Cobra standing upward! To say that Dave STOPPED in his tracks, then RAN BACKWARDS, is putting it far too mildly.

In his *own words*: "In a half stride downward (that's with one foot in the air) I came face to face with the biggest snake I ever saw—a giant Cobra with its hood spread wide and its red eyes glaring! It was raised up three feet from the ground, ready to strike! With eyeball to eyeball and my one foot already up, I put the fastest athlete in the world to shame as I made a 180° turn in mid-air and separated myself from the Cobra by a number of feet before it could bat a red eye!

"Oh, for my staff! I glanced quickly for a club or rock with one eye because my other eye never left the snake who continued to hold its ground. All close rocks were gigantic and the sticks too short.

"As I regained a little composure, the Cobra lowered and partially closed its hood. But at the slightest movement, it flared its hood and raised up HIGH— King of the Path!

"Finally, since I failed to challenge it, the snake's hood closed up and it began slithering away. Instinctively, I started to follow still looking for a weapon. An inner warning stopped me and I wondered, why in the world am I chasing this snake??

"Back on the path again, I thanked the good Lord for His divine protection, vowing *never* to climb that mountain again without my STAFF!"

We've laughed, remembering this episode. But, several days later, a teenaged missionary boy came flying into our home nearly hysterical. It turned out he had just came face to face with probably the very same GIANT COBRA!

PRAYER: Lord, sometimes we think we can handle something too big for us. Give us the good sense to STOP before we are bitten or harmed—whether it be snakes, other physical harm, or even sin. Thank You for Your watchful care over us! Amen.

69
THE DEADLY MAMBA

Read Psalm 91: He that dwelleth in the secret place of the most High shall abide under the shadow of the Almighty. Thou shalt not be afraid for the terror by night; nor for the arrow that flieth by day. (verses 1,5)

The typewriter clicked away as I prepared a prayer letter to send the folks back home.

Dave whizzed through the house grabbing a pellet gun left by a fellow missionary. It was the fiercest 'weapon' on the station. I heard him mumble "snake" as he dashed out. I dropped everything following close on his heels.

A student crowd had gathered in front of the library excitedly gazing up into a voluminous tree.

Black Mambas are the most deadly and dreaded snake found in South Africa. This one was spotted dangling high from a limb.

Curiosity drew the students much too close. These snakes can drop and move FAST through a group killing several people quickly. In fact, a black mamba had swam into a baptismal service held in a river close to our station killing five, including the pastor, before the baptismal candidates could escape from the water!

Dave feared for the kids and could only hope that pellets would kill a creature that size.

Our helpful Lord gave him opportunity for a good shot! The Mamba fell lifeless at his feet.

I snapped a picture of Dave holding it up. It was at least five feet long!

PRAYER: Dear God, we shudder over some of Your creatures! Nevertheless, snakes were not meant to be slithering or dreaded, but brought that on themselves. We also suffer the *consequences* of our wrong-doing. May we seek, instead, to live in the center of Your good and perfect will! Amen.

70
THE PINEAPPLES

Read II Samuel 23:15-17: And David longed, and said, Oh that one would give me drink of the water of the well of Bethlehem, which is by the gate!

The school was closed for mid-season break. Everyone was gone except Dave, me, and a handful of workers. But on weekends, not even workers were there.

It was Dave's custom, as Superintendent, to walk over the station every evening to check things out.

Weather was usually pleasant and the Mission Compound, so attractive that I loved to join him on these expeditions. Remember that the station was quite large—two schools, many buildings and houses, a workshop, etc., etc.

We had an enjoyable routine that gave us good exercise and priceless fellowship as we chatted along, carrying out this 'duty'.

The elementary school had a playground with swings and that was our ending point. We, as fifty-year-old 'kids', would swing facing the magnificent mountain view, praising the Lord for such an unbelievable place!

With EVERYONE away it would've seemed lonely except that there was GOD and Dave and I which was ALWAYS sufficient!

Swinging together one evening, I sensed a really strong *hunger* for pineapple which had been increasing all day!

Now we were completely alone on this thousand-acre compound. Pineapple was grown hundreds of kilometers away and there were no stores or vegetable stands to purchase anything. Yet I voiced this special craving to Dave, knowing that we could do absolutely NOTHING to satisfy my longing.

Wondering how I could forget about it, we noticed an old truck moving slowly toward us. It stopped right by the playground. We jumped off the swings and raced to it because, to our utter AMAZEMENT and DELIGHT, this truck was heaped with PINEAPPLES! The driver was selling them for ten cents each! We bought all we could carry in my skirt and Dave's arms and PRAISED ALMIGHTY GOD that He would meet such an unimportant need in such a miraculous and abundant way!

PRAYER: Dear Lord, thank You that You meet not only our needs, but often even our 'greeds'! We LOVE YOU! Amen.

71
THE MEAT MAN

O Praise the Lord, all ye nations: praise him, all ye people. For his merciful kindness is great toward us. Psalm 117:1,2a

Ngwana was a fascinating place just up the mountain road from us.

It was a market place with many people milling around. There were always those who were interested in hearing the gospel and I loved to share in that place.

One afternoon, there was a colorful African man dressed strangely with a huge, bulging, leather bag strapped to his bicycle.

He moved slowly among the groups who gathered around him, all talking at once with Emalengeni (Swaziland money) passing from hand to hand.

His hat was bright with feathers all over it, each a different color. Some hung down and some stuck up through the top.

I thought he might be a witch doctor or medicine man. I wished that I could talk with him about Jesus. I even prayed, silently, for such an opportunity.

Many people also gathered to hear the gospel that afternoon and God blessed His Word to hearts! But the strange man didn't come near and as I drove away, he was still busy with his leather bag and whatever was in it that drew so much attention.

The next day, I described him to an African friend. She laughingly explained that he was a *meat man*. His leather bag was full of freshly-butchered meat and each different colored feather stood for a kind of meat so, all could tell, by his feathers, what variety of meat was in his bag!

It was certainly different than the meat markets we have in our country. But that explained the interest and the emalengeni that was flowing!

PRAYER: Lord, You have such unique ways of meeting people's needs. Each country and culture is *different* and yet fascinating to one another. You are the GREAT PROVIDER! Amen.

72

UNTIL OUR LAST BREATH

Jesus saith unto him, I am the way, the truth, and the life: no man cometh unto the Father, but by me. John 14:6

Nomsa (my first interpreter) was studying and diligently training in a mission hospital to become a nurse.

The days were so different from the times of traveling with me in the little VW. But memories crowded in of praying together before sharing, of singing to the Lord as we would roll along, of seeing His Spirit work in the lives of people we'd witness to.

Now she was surrounded by hard work and folks who were very, very sick and even dying. She prayed hard for God to help them, knowing that only eternity would reveal the results of her toil and prayers.

As Nomsa and another nurse helped an elderly patient to a chair one day, the lady suddenly buckled, falling out of their grasp to the floor.

Nomsa called desperately, silently, to the Lord while working over her, but the woman seemed gone. Resuscitation was tried, the lady's eyelids quivered and opened. Nomsa felt as if someone else was there, not herself, as she hurriedly asked the woman if she knew who Jesus was.

"Yes," was the weak reply.

"Have you ever received Him into your heart and life?"

"No," she whispered.

Nomsa gently reminded her of Christ's saving power. God's merciful grace reached down as this patient called out to Him through the sinner's prayer, asking Christ to be her Savior and Lord!

Miraculously, she was put back into her bed and had *two more days* on this earth as a Christian before God took her to heaven to spend eternity WITH HIM!

PRAYER: Father, how we thank You, for Your mercy and grace that gives us even until our *last breath* to receive Christ! Thank You for Nomsa's gift of caring and courage for sharing! May many nurses and doctors have this kind of compassion to bring Christ to *their* patients in these days! Amen.

73
CONFERENCE TIME

For even the Son of man came not to be ministered unto, but to minister, and to give his life a ransom for many. Mark 10:45

It was The Evangelical Alliance Mission's conference time when all their missionaries would gather for business and spiritual enrichment. It was also a special week for sharing fellowship and music!

A mini children's program and field trips were planned to make it a really enjoyable and learning experience for them as well. The kids all felt like cousins. Adults were called 'aunts' and 'uncles'. It was one big happy family!

Our second year, Dave and I were asked to be cooks for that conference. There were one-hundred-twenty people attending, three full meals a day to cook and serve besides a 'tea time' each mid-morning and mid-afternoon. But twenty people were about the most I had ever cooked for at one time.

To make matters worse, the large stove at the conference grounds was broken and the only thing left to cook with were two large BLACK AFRICAN KETTLES. Yes, you guessed it—the kind you put a *real fire* under!

With three meals a day (plus tea times) to cook for 120 people and NO experience in fixing that MUCH food, especially with African POTS, we were in a 'panic' and praying DESPERATELY!

It was also our responsibility to unpack all the dishes and equipment for serving and eating as well as to purchase all the food.

God fulfilled Philippians 4:19, "But my God shall supply all your need according to His riches in glory," over and over that week as He brought an elderly lady missionary, Margaret, the very first day, who sensed our panic. She, along with her missionary partner, would report to the kitchen daily.

Margaret would ask about the menu plan for that day and also ask how I would fix this if I were home. Encouragingly she'd say, "I think we can cook the meal that way." I would look hopelessly and helplessly at those huge pots, wondering HOW??????

The menus included roast beef, swissed steak, ham, mashed potatoes, etc., etc. Margaret, amazingly, guided and helped us to prepare all those things in the African kettles, deliciously. We couldn't tell, when they were finished, that we hadn't used an ordinary stove.

At the end of the very last meal, she confided to having worked as a cook in an African hospital using these same kind of 'pots' for several years in her younger days! Had God answered our desperate prayers or WHAT??

PRAYER: Thank You, Lord, for supplying Margaret at a time of utter panic and desperate need! We still think of her as a special 'angel'. Please send Your special angels to people in great need today!

74
THE ALLELUIA!

Read Psalm 66: 1,2: Make a joyful noise unto God, all ye lands: Sing forth the honour of his name: make his praise glorious.

Singing voices resounded from the mountains of Mhlosheni daily. It was a great way to awaken and a restful way to end many days hearing the African harmony.

Somehow the idea began that WE, all of the missionaries and the African staff, should SURPRISE the students and put on an unexpected concert for *their* enjoyment. Jerry Harpool was behind it, but everyone enthusiastically joined in the plan!

It was an exciting time as we secretly, but often, began practicing the "Alleluia!" (a concert written by Bill Gaither).

The Lord somehow helped to pick the soloists (Only one couple, Marcia and Dwane Smutzer were really *talented* musically. She was a pianist and they were both gifted singers.). The rest of us could carry a tune, but the enthusiasm for doing this TOGETHER, and as a special treat for the students spurred us to surpass our normal best! It was great fun practicing and it drew us close together. These wonderful songs were heart-touching even for us as we rehearsed. Marion Albright, along with Dave and I, were the Senior members of this crew and we were given "The Longer We Serve Him, the Sweeter He Grows" to render as our special offering. We agreed so heartily with the words of this song that it was a pleasure to sing it together for the students and the Lord! The other songs were equally special whether sung together or as solos. WE WERE EXCITED!

The day finally came and we sneakily gathered BEFORE early Chapel period behind the curtains on the stage of the church. Marcia's piano had been hand-carried to this Chapel, and at a signal, stage lights went on as Marcia began playing the beautiful beginning of the "Alleluia!" The curtains OPENED and we, as if with ONE voice and heart, began singing these marvelous songs of praise! It was so exciting to see the SURPRISE and enjoyment on the faces of the 400 students!

It was a thrilling morning as each song was sung until, finally, Susan Nsibande closed singing "The Lord's

Prayer." She was an African Missionary teacher *much loved* by the kids, and her heartfelt rendition brought the students to their feet as we closed in love and praise to our GREAT GOD!!

It was *during the singing* that Dave and I remembered that this date, April 28, 1975, was the anniversary of the saddest, darkest day of our lives! It was April 28, 1960, that our third and last child was *stillborn*. Since then, every April 28th was very sad. But, THIS ONE was THRILLING! Praising God and worshiping Him in song had lifted our hearts beyond words and we could realize and KNOW again how secure and LOVED our baby, Connie, felt with Him in heaven!

We thanked and praised Him over and over as we thought amazedly how He had turned our saddest day into such an uplifting one of praise and worship! God is so very, very GOOD and WORTHY and SOVEREIGN! No wonder we can trust Him completely, even with our baby, Connie.

PRAYER: Dear Lord, we can STILL say, "THE LONGER WE SERVE YOU, THE SWEETER YOU GROW! ALLELUIA! ALLELUIA!"

75
PIPES IN THE NIGHT

Therefore, my beloved brethren, be ye stedfast, unmoveable, always abounding in the work of the Lord, forasmuch as ye know that your labour is not in vain in the Lord. I Cor. 15:58

African people over many years have developed a very cautious attitude toward foreigners, even foreign missionaries, for many reasons. So strangers are on 'trial' for a long period before being accepted or fully trusted. It may seem that one has passed the 'trial', but there is usually one *final* 'happening' that will make or break the testing.

Shabalala (the mission's night watchman), came drenched and smashing against our door during a torrential rain late one night. Communicating to Dave through Zulu shouts and hand signs, Dave somehow gathered that the main water pipe had burst up on top of the mountain.

Dressing for the rain and grabbing whatever possible to use, he followed Shabalala on the double!

The mission's water system was quite an accomplishment, designed by a missionary engineer twenty- five years before this. It started with a man-made reservoir on top of our mountain and was brought through 6" pipe *underground* by gravity down to our station where it ran a generator that supplied both schools and all buildings with drinking water and electricity.

The 'break' caused a gusher 100 feet high. Fortunately, a valve ahead of the hole could be closed. This pipe was made of cement and asbestos and there was no extra pipe like it on the station. A makeshift plumber's clamp had to be made to temporarily patch the huge break. It took one whole day of hard labor for Dave and all the workers, in the pouring rain and mud, just to make the clamp!

This kind of pipe was no longer sold or made any where in Swaziland. But after prayer, Dave, along with two men, drove a long distance to the factory which originally manufactured it. God answered prayer and enough was found (in a long forgotten storage spot) to fix our break. The owner even *donated* all pieces to the mission! God had *once again* supplied an unusual need in His wonderful way!

Two more days of hard repair work in the still torrential rain, and the job was complete with all systems 'go'.

Until this incident, we thought we were accepted and trusted by the African folks around us. But somehow there was quite a noticeable difference in the love and respect shown *after* the side by side *man's job* accomplished together with them in several days of hard labor and pouring rain! Acquaintances became dear friends which we still feel thankful for today!

PRAYER: Lord, only You know how to bridge gaps, culturally and otherwise. Draw people closer to one another and to YOURSELF! Amen.

76
HLATIKULU HOSPITAL

Read Mathew 25:34-46: For I was an hungred, and ye gave me meat: I was thirsty, and ye gave me drink: I was a stranger, and ye took me in: Naked, and ye clothed me: I was sick, and ye visited me: I was in prison, and ye came unto me. (verses 35, 36)

With people so hungry to hear about Jesus, our little VW began to travel farther and farther to spread the gospel. We named it Enqola Evangeli (after Malla Moe's donkey-drawn wagon). *Hers* was pulled by 16 donkeys; *ours* was driven by what my husband sometimes called 'lead foot'.

A group of four girls wanted to visit the government hospital, Hlatikulu, with me to sing, pray and 'share' with the patients. It was only 50 kilometers away and we arrived in high spirits.

Wondering if we would even be allowed to speak freely to patients, we prayed together, then entered timidly.

Amazingly, the hospital's Head Nurse received us *gladly*, gave full permission to go all over the hospital and asked God's blessing upon our visit!

Singing hymns as we went, our hearts were soon wrenched at the conditions we saw and the obvious needs, physically and spiritually of the patients. It was the most heart-rending sight any of us had ever seen.

And, yet, what a BLESSING, to see God take our

songs, His love and message and lift their spirits in obvious HOPE that He had not forgotten them! Many responded by receiving Christ or rededicating their lives to Him. It was thrilling to *sing hymns together with them.* They in Zulu and Siswati, we in English. It seemed as if that pitiful place was transported to heaven!

We visited every patient in every room, even in isolation as the isolated folks begged us to enter. Asking God's protection, we ministered there also!

Returning to our car, we cried together over what we had seen and praised God for guiding our visit and ministering through us!

That was the first of many such visits. God blessed every time in very special ways! Some of my 'helpers' are now nurses themselves but ALL have indelible memories of Hlatikulu Hospital!

PRAYER: Lord Jesus, thank You that You care so very much for people, especially the suffering. Help suffering people even now to know You care about them, PERSONALLY. May they commit their life to You and let You lift their heart! Amen.

77
Thengiwe

And the King shall answer and say unto them, Verily I say unto you, Inasmuch as ye have done it unto one of the least of these my brethren, ye have done it unto me. Matt. 25:40

Little did we know that our daughter Kaye's suffering from an ulcer at age sixteen, and the things we learned from that, could be used of God someday on the mission field.

In Swaziland, although fruits and vegetables grow abundantly, the main diet of the population, including our mission's school cafeteria, is 'mealie meal'. This is a course mixture made from corn, eaten together with a very rough grain bread which is usually washed down by strong 'bush' tea.

One sunny day as I walked the path to the mission's vegetable stand to buy a daily supply of fruit and veggies, I found one of our high school girls crying and in pain. As I stopped to help, she told me of her doctor's recent diagnosis of an ulcer and how she had been suffering lately, even though faithfully taking medication.

I prayed for God's divine, physical 'touch' upon her. After the prayer came a realization that God brought this girl to my attention because she might need my help.

It wasn't the first time He had put 'feet' to my prayers (personal *involvement* in His answer to a request).

The thought of the school's diet brought memory of our Kaye's need for a 'special' soft (bland) diet during her siege with an ulcer.

Thengiwe (ten-gee-we) had no possibility of eating food that could cure or, at least, help her recuperate from her illnes.

The Lord reminded me that because of our own precious Kaye, I knew what Thengiwe needed to eat, and I, personally, could cook for her IF the school officials would allow it.

They were sympathetic to this extent, that whenever Thengiwe was in *pain*, she had permission to come to me and I could fix something for her.

It was the beginning of several months of sudden 'visits' by this lovely girl.

The Lord gave us a growing friendship as we'd visit while I cooked. I enjoyed her very much, and her ulcer improved with the special attention it received. We were thankful for His healing 'touch' that we had asked for.

PRAYER: Lord, You are so GOOD in EVERY WAY! Even illness can bring blessings when we belong to You. Thank You for Thengiwe. May she live her life for You in a glorious way!

78
THE MILLIONAIRE

Jesus said . . . I am the resurrection, and the life: he that believeth in me, though he were dead, yet shall he live: And whosoever liveth and believeth in me shall never die. John 11:25,26a

Bodies of water were few in Swaziland but Dave, being an avid fisherman, had asked numerous men about fishing.

The closest place mentioned most often was Mr. Von Vissel's pond. It turned out that Mr. Von Vissel was a millionaire who owned a large, beautiful plantation on a mountain within view of our home. It was a good fishing spot, but no one was allowed to fish in his pond except by his invitation.

However, a man drove in by our mission workshop one morning on a tractor with a seat beyond repair.

Dave, who was a certified construction welder, was overseeing the workers as usual. But seeing the need, and relishing a new welding *challenge*, he soon prepared the seat, donned the apparel, and gave the seat his welder's expertise. It turned out *well* and the man was delighted! He introduced himself as Mr. Von Vissel! Then *Dave* was delighted and mentioned hearing about the 'fishing hole'. Mr. Von Vissel gladly INVITED Dave to come fishing *any time he wanted*, and Dave looked forward to that expectantly!

However, within two weeks, even before Dave was free long enough to fish, the word came that Mr. Von Vissel had suffered a sudden heart attack and was dead!

It was SHOCKING! The man was only about sixty, strong and in apparent good health with a huge estate and everything to live for. But he was here today and gone tomorrow and unable to take any of his valuables with him.

People traveled many kilometers to attend the funeral. We were there and all of the missionaries who knew him.

It was *sad* to hear the message that made NO mention at all of Jesus Christ but spoke only briefly in memory of Mr. Von Vissel and gave NO lasting comfort from God's word for the mourners.

PRAYER: God, help us ALL to live our lives for YOU and for things of ETERNAL value! Amen.

NOTE: Dave mentioned that, although he'd only briefly met Mr. Von Vissel, he wished that instead of thinking of fishing for *'fish'*, that he would have thought of fishing for *'men'* (Mr. Von Vissel in particular), but had expected to see more of this man who had even offered Dave the use of his own fishing equipment.

79
THE 'FISHING HOLE'

And whatsoever ye do in word or deed, do all in the name of the Lord Jesus, giving thanks to God and the Father by him.
Colossians 3:17

After a time, Dave wondered again about that fishing hole. Finally deciding to see about it, he drove to the Von Vissel plantation and found the head caretaker. To his surprise, the man had been told by Mr. Von Vissel that Dave had permission to fish in the pond any time! It was good news.

The 'hole' was not too big, but the fishing was

GREAT and the relaxation of it was terrific! Every once in a while he'd get to go and catch several nice bass which we'd promptly cook for a delicious dinner.

Two young Swazi students met him once with a stringer full and begged to go fishing with him *soon.*

It wasn't long 'til permission was granted, and Dave got to take them on their first fun-filled fishing trip. Both were thrilled at catching some nice sized bass and returned with an excitement like a couple of kids after their first circus trip!

When we invited them to come back that evening for their own fish supper, they could hardly believe it.

Dave and I have never seen anyone relish eating every bite of a fish meal like those two! Finally, finishing off the last bite and ending their day of 'special' happiness, they sauntered back to their 'student' world.

Other people got to enjoy that fishing hole with Dave also. It was sad to think that Mr. Von Vissel had missed the joy of sharing his 'fishing hole' with others.

PRAYER: Lord, are WE missing the joy of sharing with others? Help us to hold LOOSELY the things YOU have given us to enjoy. Amen.

80
CHICKENS IN THE CHURCH

Read Luke 17:11-19: And one of them, when he saw that he was healed, turned back, and with a loud voice glorified God, And fell down on his face at his feet, giving him thanks. (verses 15,16)

It was a bright Sunday morning at the Chapel on the mission compound. The African congregation was singing in harmony with great enthusiasm as we made our way to seats on the wooden benches.

We found no spiders crawling, bats flying, or bees buzzing as had happened on various Sundays.

However, every once in a while, we thought we heard a strange sound mixed in with the singing, along with a flopping and fluttering up on the podium.

It took a while, but finally, we heard a cackle and caught a glimpse of what appeared to be CHICKENS!

The service progressed. This time it was NOT bilingual but, though we could not understand Siswati, the spirit of worship was so precious with these people that our hearts were nourished and blessed anyhow.

It's hard to describe how a person can be blessed by a service that's not understood, but God causes it to happen and it's great!

Before the closing of his sermon, Pastor Abraham Gamedze asked for testimonies. Mrs. Zwane, the girls' hostel guardian, stood and told of her prayer to the Lord for a young son, asking for his improvement scholastically. She was ecstatic as she told of her promise to give the church several of her best chickens if he 'passed' this school year.

She said the Lord had heard and ANSWERED. Her son HAD passed and there, on the podium, was her *promised gift* cackling and flopping together!

The testimony and offering touched hearts, including ours. It was one more unusual African 'happening' that made us GLAD that God had brought us to that place!

PRAYER: Lord, it's so easy to forget promises we've made to You. Remind us *now* if there's a promise that needs to be carried out and let us know the great blessing of following through as Mrs. Zwane did! Amen.

81
GOD'S ABUNDANCE

He that spared not his own Son, but delivered him up for us all, how shall he not with him also freely give us all things? Romans 8:32

Not only was this whole Mission Station like a Garden of Eden, but even our own back yard was literally bursting with the Lord's bounty.

The Bible says that we shall eat of the fruit and vineyard which we never even planted.

Just a few steps from our back door was an orange grove (nine trees) with the sweetest oranges we had ever tasted!

A grape arbor clustered with luscious blue grapes challenged my memory of how to make jelly, *without pectin*, for all to enjoy.

Large, sweet strawberries also grew plentifully beside the grapes. The Lord's abundant supply helped us to be able to share with our fellow missionaries, some of whom were single women and one single man.

It was toward the end of our two-year term in Swaziland that the delicious strawberries were growing abundantly again. So we decided to invite all of the school's single teaching staff to lunch, consisting of sandwiches and good old-fashioned American strawberry shortcake!

It was fun preparing such a special treat for these young people who were so far away from their own parents.

We were all in the middle of this meal when Bill Nyland, the missionary who owned most of the furniture in this house, arrived to *take his table* to the station where he and his family were newly located. He was in a HURRY with a truck waiting! We all (fourteen of us) picked up our plates and stood up while Dave and Bill moved the table right out from under us! Sitting back down again on our chairs, we balanced our food the best we could on our laps and on the floor beside us.

It was a hilarious way to finish a 'special' treat!

We couldn't help but think how the Lord both 'giveth' and 'taketh' away.

Our home was used for most meetings on the station, prayer, fellowship, Bible study, business, etc. In the weeks to come, Bill kept coming to remove pieces of furniture, chairs, rugs, beds and miscellaneous. But always another co-missionary would lend what was needed for replacement.

It was really interesting to see the house change appearance every few days.

But it was also WONDERFUL to see the Lord supply through His 'family' and that we never had to stop 'hosting' meetings for lack of essential furniture!

PRAYER: Lord, Your sense of humor is *priceless*. And Your abundant supply is beyond words! Thank You! Amen.

82
JERRY AND JAN HARPOOL

He must increase, but I must decrease. John 3:30

Jerry Harpool is like a 'special' son to us and had preceded us to Swaziland to teach in Franson Christian High School.

Ten years after having dedicated our lives to serve the Lord as missionaries (if HE so desired), we were heartily involved in evangelism at home. Then, through Jerry, we discovered TEAM's need for someone like us at Franson Christian High School in Swaziland, Africa.

After prayer and preparation and wrapping things up at home, the Lord put us in His service at the school within nine months of our making application.

Jerry is a very talented, outgoing young English teacher who soon became Headmaster. He had married Jan Offett (whom he'd met while a student at Moody Bible School in Chicago). The wedding took place in Swaziland and they later had a darling little girl, Ruth, born in Zululand (they NOW have added Rebecca and Rachel to their family).

Jan is a lovely woman who more than 'handles' motherhood, hostessing, moving 13 times in 15 years and living 'on the edge' (as a missionary wife's life is described with Jerry Harpool)!

Jerry's abilities had led to a fruitful ministry with youth all over Swaziland, speaking in schools, at youth camps, even preaching in churches all over the country, as well as other occasions and meetings. He has an openness in sharing Christ as well as a transparency with himself that reaches into hearts! Their time in Swaziland was finished and much had been accomplished, but Jerry had a *few* more things he wanted to do before leaving.

One was to go with me out among the people of Mhlosheni to witness to strangers.

Taking baby Ruthie along, we drove up the mountain to a bus stop where Swazi people waited. Jerry began talking and found these people understood. They were extremely interested in RUTHIE! Holding her and touching her fair skin and strawberry-colored hair, they even lifted her dress to see her 'white' tummy. She didn't cry but her bright green eyes were large in fascination!

They held her fondly as her Daddy wisely used their interest in her to tell them of the very 'special' Child who was born to save them from their sins.

People responded to the gospel message and Jerry had the added blessing of being God's vessel among *strangers on the mountainside!*

Soon, Dave and I drove Jerry, Jan, and Ruthie to Johannesburg, Republic of South Africa airport where Ruthie took her 'first steps' just before they boarded for their flight home.

We were sad to see them leave, yet strangely GLAD that it wasn't WE who were leaving because we felt that our ministry was still not finished.

Telling of all the experiences enjoyed while serving the Lord together with Jerry and Jan in Africa would take another *sequel.* Jerry's theme of message and heart has always been that "He must increase and I must decrease."

They are STILL missionaries in Africa, now located in Capetown, South Africa, and the Lord has blessed both their ministry and their family!

PRAYER: Thank You, Lord, for the way You weave lives in and out and for the fact that Your Word tells us, "The steps of a good man are ordered of the Lord." Thank You, for all that You've done through Jerry and Jan and for the joy You gave us of serving You together with them in Swaziland. May You *continue* to BLESS their lives, family and ministry!

83

AVAILABILITY

But ye shall receive power, after that the Holy Ghost is come upon you and ye shall be witnesses unto me both in Jerusalem and in all Judea, and in Samaria, and unto the uttermost part of the earth. Acts 1:8

Many times Mr. Hutchison had spoken in the Evangelistic Bible Church of Nhlangano. It was a small picturesque place that was shared with another earlier congregation each Sunday morning.

Dave, who prefers sharing 'one-on-one' or with *small* groups, had vowed before leaving the States that he'd NEVER be able to preach.

Of course, we remembered the famous words, "Don't ever say 'never' to the Lord," and, shortly after arrival, I was thrilled to hear my husband's first sermon as I sat in the Chapel at Mhlosheni! Yes, God *could* and *did* speak through Dave in churches, schools, meetings, and various places.

It was NOT his ability but his AVAILABILITY that God honored and blessed!

Once we were even asked to preach TOGETHER at a service and somehow God even helped us to do that! Sharing became quite a challenge but also quite a blessing!

Shortly before leaving Africa, we wanted to visit the congregation at Nhlangano one last time.

Upon entering, Dave was asked to preach the morning service, but declined, not wanting to do that without preparation.

As the worship began, one layman did everything. Greetings, prayer, hymn leading, and Scripture reading were ALL led by this one dear saint. When it came time to preach he opened his Bible to Acts 1:8 and read it to the congregation.

After reading this passage, he loudly and sincerely said that he loved the Lord with all of his heart. And that was the full extent of the sermon!

We were shocked to know that this was ALL there was to a worship service in the little church whenever there was no 'visiting' speaker. Dave was hurt that he had said, "no," thinking he was not prepared to preach on such short notice but realizing now that even without preparation, GOD would have given him a message for this evidently 'hungry' congregation.

It *still* can bring tears to our eyes remembering how little one needs to know to be able to 'share' in Africa!

PRAYER: Lord. even when we feel *unable*, help us to be WILLING, with Your help, to DO whatever You bring before us! Amen.

84
THE PRAYING CHURCH

Read James 5:13-15: And the prayer of faith shall save the sick, and the Lord shall raise him up. (verse 15)

Although Dave was not one to become ill (he'd hardly ever had a sick day in his life), shortly after our arrival, he became very ill with flu-like symptoms.

Using all the usual flu medicines to help him, somehow, instead of improving, he grew weaker, was unable to eat, and could hardly stand up.

Unused to seeing Dave be anything but strong and active, I was really concerned!

One Sunday, as I for the second week had gone to church alone, many Swazis asked about him.

Later at home, I heard voices singing hymns that sounded as if they were coming gradually closer. Soon there was a knock at the door. I was really touched to see practically our whole church congregation singing outside our home. They had come to pray for Dave's healing!

A large number of them entered, knelt in our living room and prayed fervently in their language! As they finished and filed out, others came in and continued the heartfelt prayers until all had prayed on Dave's behalf.

Though very ill, he was aware of their presence and thankful for their loving concern. The compassion shown brought us closer to them in spite of the language barrier.

It was the next day that I thought of *boiling* our water even though I had been advised that it wasn't necessary because of the mission's fine water system and the fact that no one else had ever became ill from it. I was not ill either.

Nevertheless, I boiled all water in the house, including what was to become ice cubes, leaving no form of water unboiled.

Within two days Dave began to improve. By the end of another week he was strong enough to walk around and attended church the following Sunday thanking the congregation and God for answering their prayers for healing.

As long as we were in Africa and whenever we return or travel for the Lord, Dave's water must be boiled.

It wasn't until shortly *after* his illness that we discovered the serious and even life-threatening complications that 'sensitivity' to water can cause.

PRAYER: Lord, thank You for Your family, "the family of God," and the empathy and compassion for one another, no matter what race or language. WE ARE ONE!!! Amen.

85
THE BUS AT THE POST OFFICE

So then after the Lord had spoken unto them, he was received up into heaven, and sat on the right hand of God. And they went forth, and preached everywhere, the Lord working with them. Mark 16:19,20

A favorite place to share the gospel was at the bus stop across the road from the mission compound. Crowds of people would gather, waiting for busses and to go to the post office next door.

Ladies sold vegetables, fruit, handmade things and even 'fatties' (a heavy, doughy sort of doughnut hole) made right on the spot in greasy lard heated in a large can with a wood fire under it.

The busses were crowded, hurrying riders on and off in order to rush up the mountain to the next stop. Often people leaned out the windows shouting to sellers who would run to the windows selling fruit and vegetables as fast as they could.

While distributing tracts there and talking to as many folks as possible one busy afternoon, there were so many arms reaching out the windows shouting for MORE until finally, the people urged me onto the bus to give out this gospel news!

I could hardly push through the crowd on the bus, but happily tried to fill all the hands reaching for the message.

Folks tried to help, stepping on each other to make way for me to get to the end of the bus.

As I turned to start back to the only door, the bus suddenly leaped thunderingly forward in HIGH GEAR!

My heart jumped! Having no money with me and packed into the back with many people, my shouts and their shouts to the driver were unheard. Looking around, I saw everyone laughing in a friendly way. Then, shouting Siswati in unison, they were able to make the driver *wait* while they literally dragged and pushed me through the crowd to the door.

Hardly had my second foot reached the ground 'til the bus zoomed off with people waving, laughing, and even saluting as I thankfully regained my equilibrium.

From then on I always found a special welcome at the bus stop and someone would usually say they had been in the crowd or on the bus that day I nearly got taken for an unexpected ride!

PRAYER: Lord, You knew the need of the Swazi people on that bus hungry for food, but also hungry for the GOSPEL. In a humorous way, You helped me to be accepted in that place where I could minister to countless needy people in the months that followed. Thank You, and I pray that MANY found Christ after reading the gospel and that You'll help them even NOW to *live for You!* Amen.

86
GOD'S HELP WITH HOMESICKNESS

And Jesus answered and said, Verily I say unto you, There is no man that hath left house, or brethren, or sisters, or father, or mother or children, or lands, for my sake, and the gospel's, But he shall receive an hundredfold now in this time, houses, and brethren, and sisters, and mothers, and children, and lands, with persecutions; and in the world to come eternal life. Mark 10:29,30

People probably wonder how missionaries cope with homesickness and loneliness for their families left behind.

We wondered also and prayed a lot about that before we left home. Our daughter, Kaye, lived near us back home, with her husband, Ernie, and our darling granddaughter, Connie Sue, and seven-month-old, round little grandson, Mark. Our son had just been married to Vicki three weeks before our departure. How would we ever SURVIVE away from all of them was our BIG question?????

We were going to MISS them all terribly!! There was no way around that. Somehow, as we prayed, the Lord helped us to have a peace to know that we MUST go and then trust Him to help us through these things that were beyond our understanding.

As busy as we were after arrival, the 'settling in', excitement and awesomeness of such a strange, yet beautiful new world, doors and opportunities opened immediately and kept us constantly challenged. Yet, it wasn't long until one afternoon an aching restlessness filled us and trickling tears were going to be followed by a terrible attack of *homesickness.*

Literally running out of the house and into the VW, we tried to *run away* from it.

Just as the agony became unbearable and sobs were close, we noticed a young Swazi mother walking along the road with a little girl (yes, about 5 years old) and tied on her back was a 'round' baby boy of about 7 months age. We were OVERJOYED! Stopping beside them, we motioned her inside, and I held out my arms to the children. Then my lap and arms were full of these two cute kids!

We managed to communicate through odd sign language discovering that the young woman's destination was the African store close by and we headed for it. Reaching there, I somehow managed to get the baby tied to MY back and, clutching the little girl's hand too, we had a delightful time together. The Lord eased the pain and we were able to think about and talk of our loved ones again, *happily,* without agony.

It seemed that always when the homesickness would build up, the Lord would fill our house with the other young missionaries at the station and their children, especially one particular family, the Brittens: Bruce and Carol and their children, Bobby and Sue. Also, many times He would bring an opportunity for us to share with large groups of children or young people.

Whenever I was asked to teach the weekly Chapel lesson to the elementary children, there were so many kids that every bench and all of the floor space, as well as the stage, was filled with them. There was only room for my feet and the little kids COMPLETELY surrounded me. I could hardly move or breathe! It was WONDERFUL because they were so eager and *needed the message* and I needed THEM!

God always helped us in our need and kept our hearts at peace to be able to continue following and serving HIM!

PRAYER: Lord, again we THANK YOU that You met our need, and for the high school students and young children who came to us to be ministered to, but who also lovingly ministered to us. You are so FAITHFUL to Your PROMISES. We LOVE YOU!! Amen.

87
'OLD FAITHFUL'

But seek ye first the kingdom of God, and his righteousness; and all these things shall be added unto you. Matt. 6:33

All kinds of beautiful, even exotic flowers grew in Swaziland. During most of the year, the countryside was ablaze with color. Flowering trees, bushes, shrubs and plants were all along the wayside and surrounding houses.

Back at our home in Ohio, we'd kept a house plant growing for 20 years. It was a large, pink, flowering Begonia that had belonged to a favorite aunt who'd gone on to Heaven. We called it "Old Faithful" because somehow it *kept growing* even if only one leaf would remain for a 'fresh' start from the original plant. In its flowering stage it was gorgeous! We wondered, as we left everything behind, if "Old Faithful" would survive and knew it'd seem strange not to have it around.

The very FIRST thing we saw as we walked up to the house we were to occupy in Swaziland were TWO huge, pink flowering Begonias growing on both sides of the walk right next to the front stoop! They, too, were gorgeous and were GIANTS compared to our plant at home.

These bloomed nearly all year round and were a constant beautiful reminder of home and family!

PRAYER: Dear Lord, it's just like You to replace our "Old Faithful" with TWO plants even bigger and just as beautiful for our enjoyment while serving You. You are so amazing and so GOOD in *small ways* as well as GREAT and MIGHTY ways!! We thank You! Amen.

88
THE GRAVEYARD

And as Peter was coming in, Cornelius met him, and fell down at his feet, and worshiped him. But Peter took him up, saying, Stand up; I myself am a man. Acts 10:25,26

Malla Moe's name came up so often in talking with the African people. Hundreds of them had found Christ through her witness and life. Many, many of the African pastors and Christian teachers who shared their testimonies with us would tell how God had used Malla Moe to lead them to Christ. It was so thrilling to hear how God had blessed the ministry of this Norwegian woman who had loved and served Him with her whole heart! How she had LOVED the African people also!

What a testimony even now, thirteen years after her death! What an example!

We had heard much about her while at missionary candidate school, then had read her biography at Franson Christian High School. But meeting many of the people whose lives were touched by her ministry brought even more interest and inspiration. As Dave and I walked one evening, he took me to a place on the station which he had just discovered that day.

It was a strange, weedy, rundown *graveyard* with cows and chickens wandering through it.

Hidden among the weeds, we found a tombstone

with MALLA MOE's name, birth and date of death engraved. Other prominent missionaries who had served in Swaziland were buried there also.

We were aghast at the lack of care and respect for these distinguished servants of the Lord, and decided to do all we could to change that.

Weeding, mowing, painting, and erecting a little fence to surround the grave were on our list of projects to 'fix up' Malla's resting place.

The Lord always guides right, so it wasn't long until our fellow missionaries on the compound heard about our graveyard 'project'.

Fortunately, they reminded us of the African's *ancestral worship* and how confusing it is to them if they hear us preach Christ to them and yet *see us* seemingly worship OUR ancestors by beautifying gravesites and paying special tribute.

We were THANKFUL that our 'graveyard project' had NOT been started yet, so no harm was done!

The last thing Malla Moe would have wanted would've been for her beloved African people to think we or anyone else would seem to worship HER instead of JESUS CHRIST whom she loved and served so faithfully!

PRAYER: Lord, help people today to find and worship You, the only true and LIVING GOD! Amen.

89

A VISIT TO MALLA MOE'S WAGON

And they that be wise shall shine as the brightness of the firmament; and they that turn many to righteousness as the stars for ever and ever. Daniel 12:3

In Episode 13 we've written about Malla Moe and the gospel wagon used throughout her ministry. It was pulled over the mountainsides by sixteen donkeys taking her to the kraals (homes) of the African people where she preached Christ and taught them the basics of Christian living.

This wagon was kept intact at Franson Christian High School after her death. It was placed under a specially built roof shelter in such a way that it couldn't be moved.

Visitors were always interested to see it, relishing the exciting true stories of Malla's ministry. However, it was kept locked and no one could go inside.

It was such a special treat for us when Dave, while sorting and marking the many, many keys put in his charge, discovered that one of them was to Malla Moe's wagon!

Pioneer missionary Malla Moe's home on wheels that took her across Swaziland where she lived among the Africans she loved.

It was one of those school holiday times when we were alone again on the station. It had always been fun to peek in the windows, walk around it, and imagine the ACTION this relic had seen!

Amazingly, this time, Dave pulled out a key and opened the door! We walked in reverently, thrilled to see and touch this missionary's 'home' and prayer sanctuary on wheels. One of the secrets to Malla's fruitful ministry was a life FILLED with *prayer*.

Her minute size, 4'10", was evident by the tiny bunk, short table benches, etc. Although I, myself, am under 5' tall, even I could not stretch out completely on her bunk bed.

We spent the afternoon admiring and examining. What a pleasure it was to even find, in a cupboard, a few letters written by Malla, so full of her personality and heart for the Lord that reading them made her come alive.

That was such a memorable time and it was impossible to leave the wagon without spending time in prayer together. We KNEW the Lord was there. We felt as though Malla had joined us too!

PRAYER: Lord, thank You again for Malla Moe, her faith, her life and ministry for You! Please Lord, *raise up many, more like her—men as well as women in* THIS day and time, to bring great honor and glory to Your Name! Amen.

90
THE ROBBERS

You shall not steal, neither deal falsely, neither lie one to another. Leviticus 19:11

Franson Christian High School was in such a remote, undeveloped area that even the thought of crime never entered our minds.

But in these days and times, even Swaziland, Africa, could not escape that problem.

It was such a shock to hear one day, that right on our mission station, a robbery had taken place. None of us were in the habit of locking our doors since everyone living on the station was a missionary associated with the school somehow.

Talk about an uproar! We could hardly believe it and thought such a thing would probably never happen again. But within a week, it happened SEVERAL times! Then apprehension set in as we all wondered who would be the next victims and who the robber was. Swaziland police didn't seem interested and we worried about how this intruder would be caught.

Finally, after looking into every possible idea of who was behind this and coming up blank, an African teacher's home was invaded while the family actually was in their living room (called lounge).

The family was conversing when a bedroom door banged open and a young man burst through the room carrying a suitcase with their clothes and personal items streaming loosely as he sped out into the street. The Nsibande's took up the chase with Mr. Nsibande ending up literally sitting on this chap right in the road!

Once caught, the culprit turned out to be a mentally disturbed former student from Franson. What a relief it was to have it over and to know that it was NOT thieves from nearby Mozambique where rebels had robbed, terrorized, and killed people throughout that country! God was good in helping us locate the robber and then in giving wisdom as those in charge placed him in the custody of his parents (who, in Swaziland, deal strictly with their children).

As far as we ever knew, that was the end of robberies at Franson Christian High School! However, several years later upon our return to Swaziland, we found the whole country plagued with robberies and crime of every kind! Dave was even solicited to weld burglar bars on people's windows as a safeguard.

It is still sad to think that even primitive, beautiful Swaziland has succumbed to the modern ways of crime.

PRAYER: Dear Father, people all over the world need the Lord! HE IS THE ANSWER and the ONLY way to end the crime and chaos in this world! Amen.

91
THE PRISON

So shall my word be that goeth forth out of my mouth: It shall not return unto me void, but it shall accomplish that which I please, and it shall prosper in the thing whereto I sent it.
Isaiah 55:11

There were times when we were asked to share God's word at the prisons. The first time we went was a very anxious time, not knowing what to expect as far as the prisoners were concerned or even what a prison would be like.

We felt so compelled to claim God's promise in Isaiah 55:11 that we even kept our hand over the promise as each of us took turns speaking!

The prison officials never let us inside the dismal building, but gave the prisoners a choice of whether or not they wanted to attend the service and brought those interested outside the building to a large courtyard. Hundreds of hardened faces glowered intently at us!

There was a team ministering that morning, and as songs were sung and prayers offered, God's love surrounded that place and even the expressions on their faces softened noticeably.

God spoke His love through us. We could feel His heart breaking for them! His Spirit touched their hearts and many responded by asking Jesus into their hearts as an invitation was given!

It was such a dreary place even on that bright sunny day but Christ's visit transformed the gloom to HOPE as faces lit up with the transfiguration that can only come through hearing and believing in God's Word!

It was the first of many such trips to the prison and God's blessing seemed to be with the prisoners and the teams making those visits very special to all of us.

PRAYER: Lord, You do ask that we, as believers, minister to prisoners as well as the sick and needy. We thank You that You are always with us so that, when we obey You and do what You ask, the blessings are GREAT and MANY for those who share as well as those who hear Your Word. Amen.

92

THE CASINO

And Jesus answering saith unto them, Have faith in God. For verily I say unto you, That whosoever shall say unto this mountain, Be thou removed, and be thou cast into the sea; and shall not doubt in his heart, but shall believe that those things which he saith shall come to pass; he shall have whatsoever he saith. Therefore I say unto you, What things soever ye desire, when ye pray, believe that ye receive them, and ye shall have them. Mark 11:22-24

A fashionable hotel near the capital of Swaziland was known as a gambling and 'fast living' playground of southern Africa.

So much so, that rumors began to fly that another such hotel was in the planning for MHLOSHENI. In fact, it would possibly be built back to back with Franson Christian High School!

It was a horrible thought, to have THAT much worldliness next door to our vulnerable students.

Then the 'rumor' became REAL when a huge sign

was placed at the top of our mountain, next door to Franson Christian High School property. The sign told of the BIG CASINO and hotel which would be constructed soon on that site!

Twenty-one MILLION dollars had even been contributed by interested groups from nearby countries as an incentive for this easily accessible location.

Although prayers had been offered concerning this situation, after that sign was put up the prayer pressure increased immensely!

It didn't seem possible that God could allow such a catastrophe to happen to F.C.H.!

Yet, time and prayers went on WITHOUT a change; that is until two limosines with surveyors and engineers arrived one morning to take Dave up to see the layout of their plot, and discuss the water tables, etc, etc.

That evening, prayer meeting was a desperate call for God to intervene when suddenly Dave was praying agonizingly and almost angrily that Satan would NOT win this battle; that he would NOT get his filthy hands on our students through such a close enticement of every conceivable sin that curious youngsters might try! Dave fought Satan in prayer for our kids, wrestling their very lives from his grasp, nearly commanding God to at least *relocate* the hotel elsewhere for Jesus' sake! After having started in desperation, the meeting ended with a feeling of expectancy.

Foundation stakes were soon placed and the Swazi News broadcast an upcoming 'ground breaking' ceremony for the hotel.

Then, MIRACULOUSLY, Swaziland's *King Sabhouza* announced his disapproval of that location and suggested the nearby city of Nhlangano as an alternative.

We were back in the States by the time the Casino was built. Nevertheless, our hearts were thrilled upon knowing that our God STILL closes 'doors' that NO ONE can open (Rev. 3:7) and which even *millions of dollars* can't change! PRAISE THE LORD!

PRAYER: Dear God, we STILL praise Your wonderful intervention through King Sabhouza, that CHANGED an impossible situation and brought Glory to Yourself! Amen.

93

GRANNY MATHUNJWA

Read Colossians 3:1-4: Set your affection on things above, not on things on the earth. (verse 2)

Malla Moe had many African friends who, after becoming Christians, would become part of her wagon ministry entourage. One of these friends was Nomsa's grandmother, known as Granny Mathunjwa in her later years.

Granny M. had not only been a protege and close friend, but had helped Malla in her weakened, aging years almost like a 'lady-in-waiting'.

Nomsa took me to meet and visit with her grandmother, now aged and very weak herself, bodily, but such a strong and beautiful spirit! She was so frail, and lived in an extremely humble condition. But her radiant face showed a closeness to the Lord that made up for all the physical weakness. (II Corinthians 3:16)

She told of the exciting days of travel in the wagon and of countless times and even nights spent in prayer with her dear friend, Malla Moe.

Nomsa interpreted as we eagerly drank in all that Granny had strength to share.

It was a memorable visit! Granny M. was a highly respected and loved saint who was now a shut-in. There was no doubt that her eyes were now fixed upon Jesus and that all 'earthly' things had grown dim!

We were able to visit with her occasionally, but mostly we'd hear that she really wasn't very well.

How the time flew and our day of departure drew near. We were eager to see our family, yet *sad* to say goodbye to all the friends in Swaziland! Packing up finally became fulltime work.

As I filled boxes one afternoon, I heard nothing, but *sensed* a presence near. Checking around, I was amazed to find Granny Mathunjwa on our porch, standing tall and stately in spite of the cane that had helped her walk. Wrapped in her bright African blanket, she had come with a little great granddaughter (who spoke English) to bring a gift and say goodbye!

Our hearts melted at the thought of her sacrifice— not only because of the gift when she was so poor, but also because of the suffering it took for her to walk that distance.

The visit was far too short when she rose to go. Granny's pride wouldn't let her lean or hobble over the cane. Her steps were SLOW but her stature like a QUEEN'S. She was one of the first of a steady stream of *special* friends who came to hug, pray, and say GOODBYE.

PRAYER: Dear Father, bless folks today like Granny M. who've lived a long, full life of faith and service to You. Give them strength and a GREAT portion of Your comforting LOVE for each new day!

94
MY BEST FRIEND IS JESUS

Greater love hath no man than this, that a man lay down his life for his friends. Ye are my friends, if ye do whatsoever I command you. John 15:13,14

The sound of beautiful African harmony floated all over our mountainside. It was our last Sunday at the church on the station. The hymns were familiar; we could join in English accompanying their Siswati. It was always moving to sing with our African sisters and brothers in Christ the stirring songs of churches all over the world. It doesn't matter what country, race, culture, age, or language when the *tune is the same* and the HEARTS ARE ONE in Christ. The hymns are lifted right through the rafters to Heaven!

The place was packed and, as was the custom, we were to address the congregation in farewell. It was hard to say goodbye not knowing if we would ever be back. Some of the older folks (like Granny M.) would soon be with the Lord. The high school students would become leaders all over Swaziland in the near future. The congregation was growing spiritually and in numbers. We would MISS them ALL greatly! Our love went out to them!

The doors burst open and all of our young children from the Junior Church marched up on the stage. Like kids all over the world, they were too cute for words!

The most surprising and exciting thing that happened was when they began to sing to Dave and me in ENGLISH, with all their little hearts, "MY BEST FRIEND IS JESUS!"

There wasn't a dry eye in the place! So many of them had NOT known of Jesus before the Junior Church was started and NOW He was their very BEST FRIEND! God had blessed! And how we praised Him! No gift could surpass this one. Their happy eager faces and joyful voices were forever printed on our loving memories of Swaziland.

Our BEST Friend is JESUS too!!!!

PRAYER: Heavenly Father, thank You for our friends in Swaziland who found Jesus and may their faith be still 'growing' today, even the little children who are now grown up! Help someone today to find Jesus as their very best Friend in all the world!

95
WRAPPING UP

Read I Kings 17:8-16: And the barrel of meal wasted not, neither did the cruse of oil fail, according to the word of the Lord which he spake by Elijah. (verse 16)

The final day arrived. Bags were packed, waiting since dawn, while Dave and I did all we could to return the things lent to us for living these last two years—meanwhile, still saying more goodbyes on the run.

Our fellow missionaries had given us temporary use of everything imaginable. We, who had hardly ever borrowed anything in our lives, had thankfully appreciated their generosity!

It was comical as we carried even furniture back to owners on the station.

But the surprise and blessing came as we opened our food cupboards, filling boxes and baskets time after time, taking foodstuff to these friends. Over and over and faster and faster we moved to empty the shelves.

Before coming to the field, we had wondered *how* we could ever live and survive on the money allotted to us for living expense. But God had so FAITHFULLY supplied! He had stretched our money and supplies far beyond anything we could have imagined. There had not only been plenty for US but we had constantly entertained and given to others!

Finally, exhausted, with time running out, we wrote notes to leave in the house telling our friends to help themselves to all the groceries still left behind.

Amazingly, we saw and acknowledged that, although we had worked for days and since dawn *that* morning to give everything away, there was no way that we could empty those shelves!

Our God, the Great PROVIDER, had filled them,

and these supplies were NOT going to run out as long as we were still there!

PRAYER: Thank You, Father, for Your bountiful supply, guidance, care, and BLESSING to *us* and to ALL missionaries in every way!! Amen.

96
THE LAST RIDE AROUND THE STATION

Read Philippians 1:2-11: I thank my God upon every remembrance of you, Always in every prayer of mine for you all making request with joy, Being confident of this very thing, that he which hath begun a good work in you will perform it until the day of Jesus Christ. (verses 3,4,6)

George Villakati, along with Susan Nsibande, two of Franson's highly esteemed African staff, pulled up in our drive to 'collect' us as they called it for one last ride around the mission station.

The little VW was packed to the hilt ready to take us to Johannesburg where, Lord willing, we would sell it FAST, finish a few last minute details, then board our plane for home. It was time to leave!

Unaware of the 'custom' of this last ride, we, nevertheless obliged as they ushered us into the rear seat. First dashing back for a small jar, I filled it with the red sand from our drive—just a 'piece' of our Africa to take with us!

It seemed that the dream was ending and we were about to wake up to find that the trip to Swaziland had never happened!

There was no time to think about it as George drove us past the church where people were waving, then down the campus beside the school classrooms with many students hanging out the windows shouting goodbyes.

The car swerved on past the workshop and workers. Tears welled up as these dear people saluted while Mr. Robert Mamba, our beloved workers' foreman, *bowed to the ground* in a goodbye salute to Dave, his friend!

George sped to the school ground's entrance where someone waited with our VW.

A last blessing came from George as he tried to express, in his way, that the Swazis had seen what a love marriage was like through Dave and I. Swazi marriages are arranged by their parents and life for them is really different and tough.

We still feel thankful for his openness and *tribute* at that last minute. It was the FINISH of two wonderful years of serving the Lord in Swaziland!

PRAYER: Thank You, Lord, for Your BLESSING in taking us to Africa! Thank You for ALL who supported us in prayer and giving and in so many other ways! Each has had a great part in these experiences and in the rewards that we'll share TOGETHER in Heaven some day! TO YOU, LORD, BE ALL GLORY, HONOR AND PRAISE FOR IT ALL!!! Amen.